W9-DGS-592

Portrait of St. Francis by Margaritone d' Arezzo, ca.1260. Siena, Pinacoteca Nazionale. Perhaps Margaritone best captures Francis' simplicity. The artist was apparently a Francis specialist; a number of wood panel paintings of Francis by him or his followers survive. They are located in Arezzo, Rome, Castiglion Fiorentino, and Montepulciano.

THE WAY OF THE CHRISTIAN MYSTICS

GENERAL EDITOR

Noel Dermot O'Donoghue, ODC

Volume 8

Francis of Assisi

The Way of Poverty and Humility

by

William R. Cook

Michael Glazier
Wilmington, Delaware

About the Author

William R. Cook received his Ph.D. in medieval history from Cornell University. At present, he holds the rank of Distinguished Teaching Professor at the State University of New York at Geneseo. Professor Cook has taught and lectured on St. Francis throughout the United States, and has directed summer seminars on Francis' life for the National Endowment for the Humanities in Assisi and Siena.

First published in 1989 by Michael Glazier, Inc., 1935 West Fourth Street, Wilmington, Delaware 19805.

Distributed outside North America and the Philippines by Fowler Wright Books, Burgess Street, Leominster, Herefordshire HR6 8DE England.

Library of Congress Cataloging—in—Publication Data

Cook, William R. (William Robert), 1943-
Francis of Assisi/by William R. Cook.
p. cm.—(The Way of the Christian mystics;)
Bibliography: p.
Includes index.
ISBN: 0-89453-626-5
1. Francis, of Assisi, Saint, 1182-1226. 2. Christian saints—Italy—Assisi—Biography. 3. Mysticism—Italy—History.
4. Mysticism—History—Middle Ages, 600-1500. I. Title.
II. Series.
BX4700.F6C65 1989
271'.3'024—dc19
[B] 89-30011
CIP

ISBN: *Way of the Christian Mystics* series: 0-89453-630-3

Cover Design by Brother Placid, O.S.B.
Typography by Phyllis Boyd LeVane
Printed in the United States of America

Contents

For my sons, Gualberto Fernandez and Angel Quintero

Editor's Preface

Up to quite recently mystics were either misunderstood or simply not understood. But now we are coming to see that, in T.S. Eliot's words, the way of the mystics is "our only hope, or else despair." As the darkness deepens, and the lights go out, those ancient lights begin to appear and to show us the way forward. They are not only lights to guide us, but are each a human countenance in which we can recognise something of ourselves—each is a portrait for self-recognition.

Unfortunately, the great Christian mystics have been generally presented as models of perfection or monuments of orthodoxy—sometimes, too, as inhumanly joyless and ascetical. Yet they were, above all else, men and women of feeling, always vulnerable, at times perhaps insecure and uncertain of the way ahead. For all that, they all shine with a special divine likeness and a special human radiance.

Each of the following portraits tries to present a true likeness of its subject, a likeness that comes alive especially in the ordinary and the everyday. In each case the author has been asked to enliven scholarship with personal warmth, and to temper enthusiasm with accurate scholarship. Each portrait hopes to be in its own way a work of art, something carefully and lovingly fashioned out of genuine material.

The main focus nevertheless is on the way in which each mystic mediates the Christian Gospel, and so gives us a deeper, richer, clearer vision of the Christian mystery. This kind of exposition demands the reader's full and prayerful attention. Each book is the story of a pilgrimage, for the mystic, the writer and the reader.

Noel O'Donoghue

Acknowledgements

I wish to acknowledge at least some of the academic, spiritual, and personal debts I incurred while writing this book. Time to write this book was available to me because of a sabbatical leave from the State University of New York at Geneseo and from a grant from the National Endowment for the Humanities.

I have had the opportunity to learn about St. Francis while teaching about him to a variety of audiences. Both alone and with my friend and colleague Ronald Herzman, I have taught a course about St. Francis at S.U.N.Y. Geneseo. My debt to Ron Herzman is far too great to explain to those who do not know him. I had the opportunity to teach my course on Francis at Siena College in Loudenville, NY; there I benefited from the kindness and insight of the friars of that institution. I have often done research and given lectures at St. Bonaventure University; there too, I have received encouragement and insight.

In 1987, I had the pleasure of directing a National Endowment for the Humanities summer seminar for school teachers in Italy concerning the early accounts of Francis' life. Those fifteen bright and eager participants and my administrative assistant, Kathe Hartnett, provided me with many of the ideas I have presented in this book. They will know when they read this just how important their contributions were.

During numerous trips to Italy, I have had Siena as my second home and the Bianciardi family as my second family. I am grateful for their love and hospitality and their insistence that I work hard to improve my Italian. Guido Bianciardi has spent numerous hours on my behalf both while I was in Italy and during my time in the USA. He lives virtually on the spot where Francis encountered a young man more than 750 years ago; Francis' gentlenesss and joy are alive and well in Guido.

I have had many friends and students and family members as travelling companions in Italy while I have been engaged in research on Francis of Assisi. I appreciate their companionship and patience and insights. I must single out Wes and Lynn Kennison and Father Gerry Twomey for special thanks.

Although I have been aided and encouraged by many scholars, there are two who must be mentioned by name. Father Wayne Hellmann, O.F.M. Conv., invited me to St. Louis eight years ago to speak on Francis. Since that time, we have become good friends. His stories of being with Franciscan nuns in Burma for Christmas and giving a speech on St. Francis to the Indiana state legislature belong in any collection of modern Franciscan lore. Professor Ewert Cousins of Fordham University, one of the leading scholars of Franciscan spirituality, has been friend, mentor, and resource.

I owe a special debt to Father Bruce Ritter, O.F.M. Conv., founder of Covenant House in New York. I am inspired by his work and by his and his staff's compassion for hurt kids as well as their prophetic cries against those who hurt them. Meeting Father Ritter and helping to raise a little money for Covenant House in Geneseo are important parts of my involvement with those doing Francis' work today.

This book is dedicated to my two younger sons, Gualberto Fernandez and Angel Quintero. They are sometimes perplexed at my hours of labor in libraries and museums and at the word processor, but they understand full well the attraction I have to Il Poverello. He has become a part of their lives, and I am ecstatic that I can share this most sharing saint with them.

Notes Concerning Citations and Translations

The writings of Francis and many of the early lives of the saint and documents relating to his life have been assembled and translated in *St. Francis of Assisi: Omnibus of Sources* (hereafter *Omnibus*) edited by Marion Habig and published by the Franciscan Herald Press in 1973. This volume also includes a concordance of the various early biographies of the saint as well as a long bibliography.

The writings of Francis of Assisi exist in several English translations. I prefer the one of Regis Armstrong and Ignatius Brady published under the title *Francis and Clare: The Complete Works*. It is published by Paulist Press as a part of *The Classics of Western Spirituality* series. Citations in this book are to the Armstrong/Brady translation.

The earliest life of St. Francis was written by Thomas of Celano; later he wrote a second life and still later compiled a collection of miracles, mostly posthumous, associated with Francis. These works are usually referred to as I, II, and III Celano respectively and will be so cited in this book, with a chapter number following. I will occasionally use the Latin *Vita Prima* to refer to I Celano. Celano's two lives of Francis are translated in their entirety in the *Omnibus*; they have also been separately published in paperback by the Franciscan Herald Press under the title *Saint Francis of Assisi* by Thomas of Celano. Both editions of I and II Celano also contain selections from III Celano. However, there is no complete English translation.

There are several English versions of St. Bonaventure's life of St. Francis, the *Legenda Maior* (henceforth *LM*). The translation in the *Omnibus* is certainly adequate. However, I much prefer Ewert Cousins' translation in his volume for the Paulist Press' *The Classics of Western Spirituality* that contains several of Bonaventure's writings. Quotations from the *LM* will be from the Cousins translation and will include a chapter number in Roman numerals followed by a section number in Arabic numerals. Cousins' translation does not include the section of the *LM* devoted to Francis' posthumous miracles; however, they are included in the translation in the *Omnibus.*

The two other works of Bonaventure in the Paulist Press volume are also important to this study. They are *The Soul's Journey into God* and *The Tree of Life*. For the former, the citations will contain both chapter and section number, while for the latter there is only a section number.

Biblical quotations will be from the *New English Bible*, and citations will follow standard citation practices.

Introduction

Not only is St. Francis of Assisi one of the most written about Christians, but some recent books about him suggest by their titles something quite special and unique about him. Among some titles of the last few years are *The Last Christian: A Biography of Francis of Assisi*; *Francis: The Journey and the Dream*; *St. Francis: Nature Mystic; St. Francis: A Model for Human Liberation*; and *God's Fool.*[1] These and hundreds of other titles make unmistakably clear that this thirteenth-century Umbrian saint, Francesco Bernardone, is indeed someone of great importance and vitality.

Francis is known today not only because scholars and spiritual writers find him an important and attractive subject. Recently, the all-time best seller about Francis was published by Marvel Comics—*Francis, Brother of the Universe.* About fifteen years ago, Franco Zeffirelli did a film version of the saint's life called *Brother Sun, Sister Moon.* Nikos Kazantzakis wrote a novel based on Francis' life, and Umberto Eco's recent *The Name of the Rose* focuses on the question of the nature of Franciscan poverty.[2] Furthermore, Francis of Assisi is probably the non-biblical saint most often represented in Catholic art. His image has been created not only by artists of the genius of Giotto and El Greco but by countless lesser figures. And his statue can be found in numerous chapels and gardens throughout the world.

[1]The authors, respectively, are Adolf Holl, Murray Bodo, Edward Armstrong, and Leonardo Boff. Complete citations and brief annotation are in the bibliography.

[2]Full citations to these works are in the bibliography.

Francis' appeal cuts not only across centuries but across confessional boundaries. He is virtually the only saint not in the Bible whose name and image are often heard and seen in non-Catholic churches. The beginning of modern scholarship on Francis was the work of Paul Sabatier, a French Protestant; and one of the most distinguished scholars of Francis and early Franciscanism today is John Moorman, the Anglican Bishop of Ripon. The most important piece of fiction based on the life of Francis was written by Nikos Kazantzakis, who was raised in the Orthodox tradition.[3] It is no accident that in October, 1986, Pope John Paul II invited leaders of all the world's religions to come together in Assisi to pray for peace. Somehow it did not seem odd or inappropriate to see in *Time* a photograph of the Dalai Lama sitting in front of Francis' beloved little church called the Porziuncola and a Crow Indian dancing before the little chapel of San Damiano, which Francis rebuilt with his own hands.[4]

For Americans in both hemispheres, the name of Francis of Assisi and people and ideas associated with him dot our map thanks to Franciscan missionaries. Cities named Vera Cruz and Santa Cruz are reminders of Francis' special devotion to the Holy Cross. There are many cities named San Antonio and Santa Clara for the second and third Franciscan saints. Of course, there are numerous cities in the Americas named San Francisco. And Los Angeles is named for Francis' favorite church, Our Lady of the Angels, also called the Porziuncola.

Much, although not all, of Francis' appeal in the modern world is based on his love and respect for nature. Francis is rightfully the Catholic Church's official patron saint of the ecology movement. Francis is well-known for preaching to the birds, loving and taming animals, and celebrating creation in his "Canticle of the Creatures." And a friar has recently published an updated version that praises Sister Nuclear Fusion and Brother DNA.[5]

[3]See the bibliography for complete citations.

[4]*Time*, November 10, 1986: 78-79.

[5]Eric Doyle, *St. Francis and the Song of Brotherhood* (New York: Seabury, 1981), pp. 188-189.

However, there is much more to this man Francis than nature stories. Francis is the founder of an Order, now a family of orders, that bears his name; and their work is also in part responsible for Francis' fame. In the USA, for example, friars and sisters run a number of educational institutions from grade schools to universities. Many people have been cared for in hospitals named for St. Francis. Friars and sisters minister at college Newman Centers but also in soup kitchens and shelters for the homeless and on Indian reservations. One well-known American friar, Father Bruce Ritter, has become the nation's most eloquent spokesman for and protector of America's abandoned, abused, and runaway children.

All these ways in which Francis and his spirit are alive in our world are important. However, adding the aforementioned elements together falls short of presenting all the spiritual dimensions of the little poor man from Assisi. In order to discover this man and his charism, we need to return to the thirteenth-century sources. The material is at the same time overwhelming and disappointing. Compared with other medieval people, Francis is someone we know a great deal about. A collection of various documents and written accounts of his life from the hundred years or so after his death takes up about 2,000 printed pages and is by no means complete.[6] Francis has left us a fairly large body of his own writings, most notably two different rules for his Order, his "Canticle of the Creatures," some letters, and some liturgical materials. Many of the other documents were written by people who knew Francis personally or at least had talked with his companions.

However, the "real" Francis is quite elusive despite all the surviving material. With some notable exceptions, his own writings do not reveal the inner thoughts and spiritual genius of this man. Although it is true that the more one reads Francis' writings, the more one continues to discover in subtle ways their richness, they hardly compare with the writings of spiritual

[6]*St. Francis of Assisi: Omnibus of Sources.* See the note in the front of this volume for citations to the various translations of sources.

figures like Bernard of Clairvaux or John of the Cross. Certainly, they do not provide us with much insight into Francis as a mystic; for they describe neither the means through which he sought union with God nor the nature of his experience with God.[7] The biographical material is also difficult for modern readers to use profitably. Much of it is not at all like modern biography but instead falls in the genre of hagiography, whose purpose is not so much to inform as to inspire.[8] All the "lives" of Francis are also products of the turbulent years after Francis' death in which there were bitter controversies within the Order and between the Order and other elements of the Church about the nature and legitimacy of Francis' way of life. Many of the texts that tell us about Francis were written in the context of these struggles and are designed to persuade the reader of the rightness of the author's view. They are not and were never meant to be detached and objective studies of Francis and his thought.[9]

Since Francis' writings tell us relatively little about him as a mystic, we have to rely on what people who were roughly his contemporaries said about him. This is a much different situation than with many of the other figures who are subjects of books in this series. Fortunately, those who wrote about Francis were themselves men of great wisdom and spiritual insight. Francis' first biographer was Brother Thomas of Celano, a gifted writer who had some personal acquaintance with the saint. His writings are of very high quality, and his stature as a spiritual writer has only recently begun to be recognized by medieval scholars.[10] The

[7]The most useful introduction to the writings of Francis is found in the Paulist Press volume *Francis and Clare: The Complete Works*. There is a general introduction to Francis' writings and also a brief introduction to each individual text. The authors, Regis Armstrong and Ignatius Brady, are among the most eminent Franciscan scholars in the world; and they are reliable guides to these important sources.

[8]There are introductions to all of the sources in the *Omnibus*. Ewert Cousins' introduction to his translation of three of Bonaventure's works in the Paulist Press volume is excellent.

[9]The best treatment of those controversies involving the Franciscans in the thirteenth century is in John Moorman, *A History of the Franciscan Order from its Origins to the Year 1517* (Oxford: Clarendon Press, 1968), passim.

[10]For a good discussion of Celano's literary genius, see John Fleming, *An Introduction to the Franciscan Literature of the Middle Ages* (Chicago: Franciscan Herald Press, 1977), pp. 36ff.

most important biographer of Francis was St. Bonaventure, a Minister General of the Order and a great philosopher, theologian, and mystic.[11] His *Legenda Maior* became the Order's official life in 1266 and has remained the best-known version of the life of Francis. Bonaventure also composed *The Soul's Journey into God*, integrating Francis' mystical experiences into the larger tradition of Christian mysticism. In addition, we have some of the writings of Brother Leo, perhaps Francis' closest companion, as well as several other accounts that were written in the thirteenth century or at least derived from early traditions.[12]

There is another kind of thirteenth-century source for understanding the life of Francis of Assisi, but scholars rarely make much use of it. In less than a century after Francis' death, there were thousands of works of art whose subject is St. Francis. From Italy alone, more than one hundred fifty paintings of the saint survive from the thirteenth and early fourteenth centuries. Of these, more than a dozen are narrative cycles containing between two and twenty-eight stories from the saint's life. Although the great majority of the stories represented are derived from written accounts, they are themselves interpretations of the stories rather than simply "copies" of the written sources in a different medium. Furthermore, both the choices that patrons and friars made concerning which stories should be represented and also what visual traditions were used in determining the way the stories were represented are themselves significant for understanding how contemporaries and near contemporaries of the saint understood the events in Francis' life.[13]

[11]There are several good introductions to Bonaventure's writings. Ewert Cousins' works listed in the bibliography as well as his introduction to his Paulist Press volume of three of Bonaventure's works are particularly valuable.

[12]Most of these other early lives are in the *Omnibus*. They include the *Legend of the Three Companions, Legend of Perugia, Mirror of Perfection,* and *Little Flowers.*

[13]At present, there is no adequate study of these paintings from the perspective of the history and development of the Franciscan Order and Franciscan spirituality. My article in a forthcoming volume in honor of my mentor Brian Tierney (*Popes, Teachers and Canon Law in the Middle Ages* ed. James Ross Sweeney and Stanley Chodorow. Ithaca: Cornell University Press, 1989) is a brief discussion of some of the relationships between the written and visual sources. I have recently finished a book that examines all the surviving Italian paintings of St. Francis before ca. 1310 and relates them to the major

My task in the pages that follow is to rely as much as possible on both written and visual sources, although I obviously must consider the discoveries and insights of modern scholarship, in order to present Francis of Assisi as a major figure in the mystical tradition. This means I will not be much concerned with Francis as the founder of a religious order. I will not present a detailed biography, although the first chapter provides a general overview in order to make the more detailed discussions of his spirituality more intelligible. Rather than attempt to discuss all texts by and about Francis of a mystical nature, I shall instead focus on six elements of his life and spirituality—his conversion; his relationship to the created world; the creation of the Christmas crib at Greccio; the role of learning; the relationship between the active and contemplative life; and his stigmatization at LaVerna in 1224, two years before his death. I believe that a detailed discussion and analysis of these aspects of Francis' life will best introduce the reader to Francis of Assisi. There is a conclusion that both summarizes the contents of the book and suggests some of the implications of Francis of Assisi's contributions for Christians at the end of the twentieth century. Finally, there is an annotated bibliography that will lead the interested reader to both the sources and some major works of modern scholarship.

events of Franciscan history and the main trends of Franciscan spirituality. I anticipate that this study, *The Early Images of St. Francis in Italian Painting*, will be published soon with numerous photographs and a comprehensive bibliography.

1

An Overview of the Life of Francis of Assisi

Lady Pica gave birth to a baby boy probably in the year 1182 while her husband Pietro Bernardone was away on business, and she named him John. When Pietro returned, he decided to change his son's name to Francesco. This took place in the small and not particularly important town of Assisi, located on the lower slope of Monte Subasio in Umbria. No one could have known that this boy would become perhaps the most important and loved saint since biblical times or that Francis' name would be used by thousands of parents for their children and thousands more by "adoption" into the family of religious orders that bear his name. And no one could have guessed that Assisi would become one of the most famous towns in the world, not because of its ancient ruins or modern commerce but because of little Francesco Bernardone.

It is a commonplace to say that Francis was born at a time of great changes in Western Europe and especially Italy; however, that hardly suffices either as a context for his life or an explanation of his contributions to Christian history and spirituality. Nevertheless, a certain amount of historical background is important in order to comprehend the physical, institutional, and mental world that Francis was born into.

It is best to begin with a brief description of the human condition at the time that Francis became a part of it. At the end of the twelfth century, probably ninety percent of the people living in Umbria and everywhere else in Europe were directly engaged in agriculture. And the ten percent who were not, including the Bernardone family, were much closer to the world of nature than are most modern city dwellers. A flood or drought or early freeze or animal disease profoundly affected every aspect of urban life. Not only did the price and availability of food fluctuate a good deal from place to place and season to season, but a city's economy and Pietro's cloth manufacturing depended on the wool and dyes that were produced. Nature was much less under human control then than now. From time to time, modern people are forced to recall the helplessness of humans before the forces of nature when there is a drought or famine or volcano or tornado. But we can light the dark, warm our houses, refrigerate our food, and produce clothes not made of animal skins or hair or plants. There were many fewer people living in Assisi and the area around it than there are today, and there were many more wild animals. There may be those who doubt that Francis actually made a pact with a wolf that terrorized the citizens of the town of Gubbio, but we should all recognize that there were wolves that needed pacifying. Despite all this, Umbria was and still is a land of extraordinary beauty. Only rarely today are there days as clear as most were in the Middle Ages, but on those days one can from Assisi see the summit of Monte Subasio, the valley of Spoleto and mountains beyond it, and the rolling hills toward Perugia. No one who has stood beneath the city of Assisi in the spring and gazed at it surrounded by the brilliant red poppies can forget that experience.[1]

There were many more people in terms of percentage of the population who appeared to be horrible to those who were fortunate. We can only speculate how many people were missing limbs and teeth, how many were deformed and disfigured from birth, diet, disease, war, or accident. Many injuries and diseases that today are minor inconveniences left permanent marks on

[1]The best description of the Umbria of St. Francis is Arnaldo Fortini, *Francis of Assisi* tr. Helen Moak (New York: Crossroad, 1981). Fortini's book at times appears to be as much about Assisi as about Francis. A shorter and less complex introduction is Raphael Brown, *The Roots of St. Francis* (Chicago: Franciscan Herald Press, 1981).

people in the Middle Ages. Most horrible of all were the lepers. Their grotesqueness and smell brought disgust to many who saw them, and it was commonly believed that the disease was God's punishment of its victims.

To get a good idea of what sorts of people one might see at the gate of a town or in its streets and churches, one can turn to the posthumous miracle stories associated with saints like Francis. In Thomas of Celano's first life of Francis, written only two years after the saint's death, he describes cures of a girl whose head had grown down into her shoulders (127), a boy whose leg was bent back (128), a boy whose knee clung into his chest (130), a man whose legs were full of sores (131), a girl who could move only her tongue (134), blind people (136), a woman subject to terrible frenzies (138), a man who vomited blood (139), a woman with a withered hand (141), a man with an arrow lodged in his eye socket (143), a man who had to wear a truss (144), several lepers (146), and several without hearing (147-150).

Of course, there were also people of great wealth who wore luxurious garments, occupied grand though drafty houses, and lived from the labor of others. Bishops and abbots too lived in great contrast with most of the population as well as with the Shepherd whose staff they carried. And the rich and poor were all mixed together in certain ways, for Italian cities were not and still to a great extent are not divided into neighborhoods on the basis of economic status. A splendid palace often was surrounded by rickety buildings where the poor dwelt. However, I doubt the contrast is any greater in twelfth-century Assisi than it is in modern midtown Manhattan where the theatre crowd and the street people pass each other every night.

During the years Francis lived (1182-1226), the economic and therefore social life in Assisi and Italy were rapidly changing. Cities such as Pisa and Venice were already wealthy and cosmopolitan thanks to their merchants and their fleets that gave them access to the eastern Mediterranean. Inland cities such as Florence and Siena were not yet as prominent as they were to become in the next century, but they were in the process of developing the political and social institutions that we associate with them. Assisi was small compared to the emerging cities in Tuscany but was nevertheless experiencing on a smaller scale many of the same problems as its neighboring cities to the north. There were merchants who were becoming important people of the town even though they were neither clerics nor large landholders, the two groups who had traditionally wielded power. Thus, new conflicts within a city and its surrounding territory were added to traditional ones. There was also a great deal of inter-city rivalry over issues of power and of pride.[2] And there were still larger contexts for rivalry and fighting, for the papacy and the Holy Roman Empire were often engaged in verbal and/or military hostilities.[3]

Assisi was the seat of a bishop and traced its Christian heritage to a missionary and martyr named Rufinus, who was the patron of the cathedral where Francis was baptized. During the eleventh and twelfth centuries, the papacy had emerged as a great world power both in ecclesiastical matters and at least what modern people would regard as purely political affairs. There were churches everywhere; in Rome at this time there was one church per eighty inhabitants. Tourists are often struck today when visiting Italian cities that there are so many churches. In addition to a cathedral, there were parish churches, chapels, and churches belonging to religious orders. And there were also many churches, some poor and even abandoned, scattered throughout the countryside. The Church performed many functions in medieval society that it is no longer responsible for. It marked the hours, decided which days were work days and which holidays, had virtually a monopoly of education, was by far the chief patron of the arts, adjudicated numerous cases in its courts including probate and all cases involving clerics.[4]

[2]The best examination of the development of a money economy for those interested specifically in Francis and the Franciscan Order is Lester Little, *Religious Poverty and the Profit Economy in Medieval Europe* (Ithaca: Cornell University Press, 1978).

[3]An excellent overview of the conflict between Empire and papacy is found in Brian Tierney, *The Crisis of Church and State, 1050-1300* (Englewood Cliffs, NJ: Prentice-Hall, 1964), esp. pp. 97-138. The book contains key primary sources as well as Tierney's analysis.

[4]For a somewhat more detailed discussion of the Church in the twelfth century, see William Cook and Ronald Herzman, *The Medieval World View: An Introduction* (New York: Oxford University Press, 1983), pp. 225-293.

Although the Church controlled religious education, it was hardly a secret that many clerics lived lives quite different from those of Christ and his apostles. Martin Luther was not the first to juxtapose Christ washing the apostles' feet with people kissing the pope's feet. Criticism of the state of the ecclesiastical hierarchy as well as parish priests and monks took many forms from mild anticlericalism to radical protests. During the twelfth century, there were preachers appearing all over western Europe who called for reform; that could mean anything from the restructuring of the institutional church to the call to a local cleric to expel his mistress. While many of these voices were lone figures, there were several movements that were well-organized and at least two that can be called international—the Albigensians or Cathars and the Waldensians.[5] In the last years of the twelfth century, there were attempts to crush these organized movements, but they met with little success.

It was into this world that Francis of Assisi was born. We know nothing specific of his childhood. He attended a school at the church of San Giorgio and learned to read and write Latin. He presumably had a "normal" childhood for the son of a wealthy merchant, perhaps travelling at least short distances with his father and observing how the business operated.

As a young man, he was quite popular with the other youths of the town. He enjoyed drinking and singing with friends and had a rather extravagant entertainment budget. He was interested in becoming a soldier. It is important to realize that for several reasons, Francis would have seen this as a "glamorous" career. First, the warriors traditionally came from the landholding class; to become a knight would have been a step up socially from being a cloth merchant. Second, Francis no doubt knew tales of great warriors of the past both real and fictional, and he loved the songs

[5]The best treatment of the Waldensians and Cathars is Malcolm Lambert, *Medieval Heresy: Popular Movements from Bogomil to Hus* (London: Edward Arnold, 1977), pp. 39-91. For an examination of these groups as part of the context of the Franciscan movement, see Rosalind Brooke, *The Coming of the Friars* (London: George Allen and Unwin, 1975), pp. 63-74. Brooke also provides some contemporary documents about the Cathars and Waldensians.

of the troubadours which glorified the warrior class in pursuit of a beautiful woman as well as in battle. And it was patriotic to be willing and even eager to take the field to defend his city against the hated neighbor Perugia. That is in fact what Francis did; however, instead of coming home to reap the rewards of victory, he became a prisoner of war in a Perugian dungeon (II Celano 4).

After his release, he became ill. Perhaps defeat and illness combined to cause Francis to do some serious thinking. Despite these setbacks in his life, he still had a rosy future. There would be other opportunities to go off to fight for a good cause. And there was always the cloth business of his father that would provide for his earthly needs. The problem for Francis was that these prospects no longer made him happy. Francis began to do things that probably seemed as strange to his father as they do to us. He went into the wilderness to pray, once changed clothes with a beggar and begged, showed deep concern for those less fortunate than himself, and even rebuilt crumbling churches. His father was furious and his mother perplexed. When Francis began to use profits from the sale of his father's cloth to buy building materials for his renovation projects, his father had had enough of this nonsense. He sought to disinherit Francis and to get all his property back. In the presence of Bishop Guido, Francis returned to his father *everything* that Pietro had given him—down to and including his underwear. This was the year 1206; Francis was twenty-four years old (I Celano 15; II Celano 12; *LM* II, 3).[6]

The next three years were ones of discovery and direction. He had rejected lots of things; what precisely was it that he was embracing? He lived in utter poverty and destitution and had to learn to accept scraps of food as his dinner, discarded garments as his clothes, working at menial tasks and begging, scorn and ridicule from both strangers and former associates, a stone for a pillow. He spent a lot of time with lepers and cleaned their sores and kissed them. All this made him happy! He walked through the woods singing songs about God, rewritten versions of trou-

[6]See Richard Trexler's forthcoming, *Naked Before the Bishop: The Renunciation of Francis of Assisi in Literature and Art.*

badour songs he had sung many times before. He prayed a lot and sought guidance from scripture. He practiced rigid asceticism. To most people in Assisi, Francis simply appeared to be insane. However, gradually other men from around Assisi asked to join him; and they wandered the countryside working, begging, singing, and calling on people to repent and be reconciled to God. Some thought they were mad; others accused them of heresy.

When their number reached twelve, they decided, perhaps at the urging of those who feared they would be treated as heretics, to seek the pope's approval of their life. It was only slightly easier to get an audience with Innocent III than it is with John Paul II. However, Francis and his brothers did see the pope. What Francis and Innocent talked about will never be known, but that conversation was, in retrospect, one of the most important in the history of Christianity. Francis wanted a simple rule, made up mostly of scriptural passages, approved. Innocent may have asked about the brotherhood's patrons. "We don't have any patrons, Holy Father." The pope probably asked about their monastery. "We sleep in barns and outdoors, Holy Father." Since they asked permission to preach, the pope would have wanted to know about their education. "I'm not a priest and none of us has attended a university, Holy Father." Innocent would have been interested in how Francis screened and tested new brothers. "Whoever wants to live the gospel life just comes with us, Holy Father."[7] Presumably, these answers were distressing to Innocent, a great legal mind. Still, Innocent granted Francis' request and established what we now call the Franciscan Order. There were several reasons for this unlikely decision. First, all Francis and his brothers were asking was to live the life of the apostles. If the pope

[7]I have borrowed these few lines rather closely from a lecture delivered by Brian Tierney. A few years ago, I took some students to a Benedictine monastery for a weekend. Tierney had been there not long before us, and the brothers asked if we would like to hear a tape of his lecture. I listened at least in part in a nostalgic mood because Tierney had been my dissertation director years before at Cornell. While enjoying this encore, I noticed that my students looked perplexed and then disturbed. They had heard me give a very similar lecture including the same imaginary conversation between Francis and Innocent III. I realized only then how much I owed to Tierney, and I want to make amends for a great deal of respectful "plagiarism" in my classes by giving him credit here.

said no because it was impractical, he would be denying the possiblity of doing in his day what all Christians claimed to be trying to do—following the teachings of Christ. Second, the heretical groups in Italy and France based some of their appeal on the claim that they rather than the followers of the pope were living the life Christ prescribed. Having these brothers live that life while in obedience to Rome would weaken the heretics' criticism of the Roman church. These reasons are of the kind historians are comfortable with. However, we should not underestimate the impression that Francis' humility and charisma made on Innocent. In part, Innocent was no doubt relying on his discernment that Francis was a man of great spiritual gifts who was not interested in power or influence but only service.

The next decade was one of enormous growth for the Order, and certain changes were called for including periodic meetings or chapters to discuss the affairs of the Order. The friars spread beyond Italy during this time. Although many of the friars were simple men like Francis and most of his earliest followers, others entered who were well-educated or who desired further education. More priests joined the Order as well. Although the Order's affairs no doubt took a good deal of Francis' time, he maintained his life of asceticism, extreme poverty, preaching throughout the Italian countryside, and prayer. He also helped a remarkable young women from Assisi named Clare to establish a Franciscan life for women, and he created a modified Franciscan life for those living in the world, called the Third Order.[8]

In 1219, Francis went to the Holy Land and preached to a Muslim sultan. While he was away, problems within the Order came to the surface. There were friars who did not join the Order to sleep in barns and do manual labor, and there were strong differences of opinion about what it meant to be a Friar Minor. And the Rule that may have been adequate for a dozen men in 1209 was not suited to the Order a decade later. Francis returned

[8]For the development of the Friars Minor, Clares, and Third Order at this time, see Moorman, pp. 32-52.

to Italy and wrote a rather long rule; some friars thought it too strict, and others found the language not precise enough. Francis went back to work and prayer and wrote a rule that was approved by Pope Honorius III in 1223. However, these years after his return from the Holy Land were difficult for Francis in many ways. He seemed out of touch with his own Order or at least with a significant number of friars. Many wanted privileges while he still found great joy in the most humble circumstances and tasks. He would ask a bishop if he may preach in his diocese; some friars wanted papal bulls that granted them authority to preach anywhere. Francis was also a sick man. He had severe eye problems as well as other debilitating diseases. His suffering was intense both in body and spirit. Yet he never lost the joy he had found at the time of his conversion. He composed his wonderful "Canticle of the Creatures" and celebrated Christmas in a new way at Greccio.

Francis more and more realized that in his suffering, he was in fact experiencing what he wanted most—to share Christ's life, which included his suffering. Christ's apostles often understood little of what He said, and one of them betrayed him. Christ's agony in the garden of Gethsemani and his passion became increasingly a part of Francis' experience. The intimacy between Christ and Francis culminated at LaVerna in 1224 when the saint had imprinted on his body the five wounds of Christ, the stigmata.

When Francis came down from the Tuscan mountain bearing Christ's wounds, he wished to return to doing what had filled him with greatest joy—caring for the lepers, begging, calling on people to repent. But he was too ill for much of that. Blind and near death, he returned to Assisi in 1226 to die at his beloved Porziuncola, one of the tiny churches he had rebuilt twenty years earlier. There, naked, he died on the evening of October 3, 1226. In less than two years, he was canonized by his old friend Cardinal Ugolino, who had ascended the papal throne as Gregory IX.

Assisi immediately became a pilgrimage site, and the splendid Basilica that now dominates the skyline of Assisi was begun in 1228; two years later, his body was transferred there from its first resting place in San Giorgio. In the next hundred years, that church received numerous visitors from popes to lepers, much as it does today. It was decorated by an extraordinary group of artists including Cimabue, Giotto, Simone Martini, Pietro Lorenzetti, and a host of others including both painters and window-makers from beyond the Alps.

The Order continued to grow and change during the course of the thirteenth century. Some changes appeared to be necessary simply because of the size and dispersion of the friars. Others were made because the papacy wished the friars to take on greater responsibilities in the Church. Francis had not wanted any of his friars to be bishops; however, in the thirteenth century, friars were called to episcopal sees in missionary areas and also in Western Europe. One was elected pope in 1288. Other changes involved the desire and need for more education for friars. In order to study at the universities, friars needed a certain stability of lifestyle; they could not be expected to study theology while begging alms or earning their daily bread by manual labor. Undoubtedly, some of the changes that occurred can legitimately be described as laxness on the part of many who entered the Friars Minor. They should not surprise us. As one historian has said, "It is not surprising that there were not 10,000 Francises, but rather it is a miracle that there was one."[9] Many of the friars including most of Francis' closest companions deeply resented the changes regardless of the reasons for them. In the years immediately after Francis' death, this "opposition" was not organized. By the end of the century, however, the minority of friars who believed in literal imitation of Francis became a faction within the Order which historians call the Spirituals. It is not appropriate here to discuss the complex issues that formally divided the Spirituals from the majority of the friars, the Conventuals. Suffice it to say that as the popes became less patient and tolerant with the Spirituals, they in turn became less concerned with obedience to the Roman see. In 1327, the Spirituals

[9]This is another phrase borrowed from my mentor Brian Tierney.

and their teachings were condemned by Pope John XXII.[10]

Not only were there bitter conflicts between groups of friars, but there was considerable opposition to the Franciscan Order from outside. Along with the Dominicans, the Friars Minor performed tasks in the Church traditionally done by secular clergy. Furthermore, the popes granted privileges to the friars that weakened the role of bishops in their dioceses. When friars demanded certain privileges at the University of Paris in the 1250s, there was a revolt by the secular masters. In addition, the friars were vulnerable to attack because two of their early ministers general, Elias and John of Parma, had been accused of heresy.

Here, then, is a brief overview of the life and times of Francis of Assisi. He lived in a turbulent age, but then so does everyone. Many biographers try to explain Francis of Assisi as a man of his times. Here is the son of the rich merchant who rebels against his father and his values. He is not unlike the sons and daughters of corporate executives who marched in the 60s or try to save whales in the 80s, it is said. But clearly we cannot argue that because Francis' father was a rich, clever businessman, his son talked to birds and wore rags. That would be to ignore the thousands of merchants' sons who accepted their fathers' values and took over the family business. Pietro Bernardone's beliefs and activities are an important context but not a sufficient explanation for Francis' life. Without ignoring the social context, we need to try to understand Francis by coming to him from another direction. We must try to discover what is different about Francis, what experiences and insights led him to renounce in such a radical way the values that had made Pietro Bernardone a successful merchant and young Francis a man of style and leisure.

[10]This clash between the papacy and the spirituals during the pontificate of John XXII forms a major part of the backdrop for Umberto Eco's wonderful novel *The Name of the Rose*.

2

The Conversion of Saint Francis

One day in the year 1206, a strange event occurred in Assisi. A young man appeared before the bishop because his father wanted back money he had been accused of stealing. When the bishop explained that the young man should return the money even if he stole it in order to do good deeds, he not only returned the money in question but stripped himself completely naked and returned to his father all the clothes that had been provided for him. From now on, the young man said, I no longer think of you as my father but only of our Father who is in heaven.[1]

Like many other great saints, there was a dramatic moment in which Francis broke from his attachment to earthly things and chose instead those things that are lasting. The story of Francis stripping himself naked is every bit as memorable as the great conversion of Augustine in a garden in Milan or Antony going off to live in the desert. However, in isolation, stories like these tell us very little. First, we need to know what occurred before, what led up to that dramatic event. What led Francis to turn away from earthly things? How did he know what to turn *to*? We also need to know what came after, for conversion is a continuing process rather than a single event in a person's life.

[1]This is one of very few stories that all three early lives, I and II Celano and the *Legenda Maior*, recount: I Celano 15; II Celano 12; *LM* II, 3. My reconstruction of the event draws from all of these texts plus the account in the *Legend of the Three Companions* 19. There are also representations of this story in thirteenth-century paintings in Florence, Siena, Assisi, and Gubbio. I am indebted to Professor Richard Trexler for letting me read his forthcoming book *Naked Before the Bishop: The Renunciation of Francis of Assisi in Literature and Art*.

Detail of Francis stripping naked before the bishop by a follower of Guido da Siena, ca.1290. This is one of eight scenes on a wooden altarpiece originally painted for the church of San Francesco in Colle Val d'Elsa, now in the Pinacoteca Nazionale in Siena. Francis, wrapped in the bishop's cloak, looks back toward his father and the worldly goods he has returned to him. Bishop Guido, representing the Church, cares for and protects the young and defenseless Francis.

Our best sources for the early life of Francis are the two lives of Thomas of Celano and the *Legend of the Three Companions*. In addition we have Bonaventure's interpretation of the early events in Francis' life. It is also necessary to use the imagination a bit to fill the many gaps in the source material. Historical imagination is not the same as either fiction or fancy. It involves a knowledge of the sources, awareness of the world in which Francis lived, and deductions about his early life from what occurred later in his life.

Young Francis grew up in the family of a hard-working, no-nonsense merchant. Competition was every bit as cutthroat as it is today in the business world, but there was no insurance policy to fall back on. Families that went broke did not file for reorganization under bankruptcy laws or sell off the Jaguar; they were forced to beg in the streets. Both parents were apparently willing to indulge Francis in his expensive and occasionally bizarre tastes. Nevertheless, from the point of view of Pietro Bernardone, his son just did not understand the value of money. He was generous with the poor and a spendthrift. He bought expensive clothes and funded feasts and drinking bouts. And he was filled with the songs and the values of the troubadour poets of southern France. He knew the tales of the Round Table and of Charlemagne. He accepted courtesy as one of the chief virtues. He probably dreamed of romance. He certainly hoped to become a knight, for the world of the troubadours was one of knights not cloth merchants.

None of this strikes us today as particularly unusual. Young men whose fathers have labored hard for their worldly goods often are more interested in the fruits than the labors, and dream of a more ideal world and their place in it.

Francis' first big chance came at the age of twenty when once again Assisi and Perugia were at war. However, Francis ended up as a prisoner of war. The sources tell us that he remained cheerful and courteous in captivity, and there is no sense that he realized the folly of war at that time.

After his return to Assisi, he became ill. As he recovered, he discovered that something was wrong. As Thomas of Celano put it,

> But the beauty of the fields, the pleasantness of the vineyards, and whatever else was beautiful to look upon, could stir in him no delight (I Cel 3).

Given what we know of Francis' later relationship with the flowers and birds, this passage suggests that Francis was depressed and perhaps vaguely aware that something was wrong. And for those who know the captivating beauty of Umbria, it is clear that his lack of delight in the beauties of nature is more than a matter of being in a bad mood.

However, he still dreamed of military glory and fame and all the privileges in society that went with those things. He jumped at the opportunity to join Walter of Brienne to fight in Apulia against the forces of certain German princes. He did not get very far. In Spoleto, he had a vision that led him to return to Assisi and wait for God to tell him what he should do (I Cel 7). He had by this time already perhaps sensed that even victory in battle and the spoils that go with it would not make him once again enjoy the fields and vineyards. He had a problem all right—and an enemy—but fighting in Apulia would not solve his problem, and the soldiers he would face there were not the enemy.

After his abrupt return to Assisi, he continued to spend time with his old friends. But while Francis would still go drinking with his buddies, he also began to pursue other things. He had always been generous to the poor and had even occasionally had clothes made that combined expensive materials with common cloth. Even in the excesses of his youth, we thus have evidence that he wished in some fashion to identify himself with the poor. He probably had not the slightest idea why he wanted to do this. But after his return to Assisi, he became more generous with the poor, at times going so far as to give a beggar part of what he was wearing. He also began to buy little objects used in churches and to send them to poor priests. Maybe at this time he began to realize that both these activities were really the same—giving to God. Francis also began to pray fervently, often in lonely places. This is significant. We must remember that in Francis' time, virtually everyone was a Christian and attended mass and prayed both in and out of church. No doubt, much prayer was mechanical and viewed as obligation. It was often performed amidst the splendor of works of art, Gregorian chant, and rising incense. And Francis never criticized this at all. But on Monte Subasio, in lonely caves, he prayed in a different way. The images of the holy around him there were not painted icons or sculpted capitals but rather the stones and trees and birds.

As Francis became more "religious," he decided to journey to Rome. At the shrine of St. Peter, he was so moved by being in the presence of the one to whom Christ entrusted his flock that he threw a lot of money through the grate in the altar (II Cel 8). That is a thoroughly comprehensible response for the son of Pietro Bernardone. In fact, Pietro might have done the same had he come to Peter's shrine in a "weak" moment. But what followed was not something Pietro would have done. Francis noticed the beggars outside the church as he was leaving. Then, he borrowed (or exchanged) clothes from a beggar and began to beg for alms. No longer was he wearing a bit of common cloth sewed to his finery; he was dressed in the grubby rags of a poor man. More astonishing than the fact that Francis did this is that he was filled with joy. We must not treat this event either as a Halloween-like masquerade or as a "black like me" experiment. This was neither game nor research. What led Francis to this extraordinary act, and why was it a joyful experience? At a time of Francis' life when the things that should have made him happy (by the world's standards) failed to do so, it is perhaps useful to do something radically different in order to discover what precisely it is that is important and enriching. Perhaps his "natural" reaction literally to throw money at St. Peter brought him no solace or feeling of grace. Maybe he saw the irony of throwing money on the grave of a man who once said to a beggar, "Gold and silver I have none, but what I have I give you" (Acts 3:6). At one and the same time he became both Peter and the beggar on the porch of San Pietro.

The joy Francis felt that day may be related to the gratefulness he felt when given even a small coin. Perhaps it occurred to him that everything he had, even his very existence, was a gift. Perhaps there was also a certain brotherhood he discovered with the other beggars that was absent from his own friends in Assisi who enjoyed his style and his largesse.

Still, Francis was not sure whether these new feelings were genuine; and he kept his begging in Rome a secret when he returned home. What we can see in these events is the process of certain instincts Francis had being transformed and purified by grace.

At this point, Francis began to understand that the roadblock to happiness was not put up by his father or anyone else but was in fact internal. Francis had a great fight to conduct, but not with members of a rival army—Francis had to conquer himself. Despite Francis' compassion for the poor, he was pampered and something of a prig who avoided things and people that were ugly. In particular, Francis found lepers to be repulsive and would not go near them. Francis recalled this on his deathbed:

> While I was in sin, it seemed very bitter to me to see lepers. And the Lord Himself led me among them and I had mercy upon them. And when I left them that which seemed bitter to me was changed into sweetness of soul and body.[2]

One day while Francis was journeying near Assisi, he saw a leper; repulsed at first, he struggled to show him compassion. He gave the leper money, kissed his hand, and offered him the kiss of peace. In some versions of the story, when Francis looked back, the leper had disappeared (II Cel 9). The point of this story is clear; what Francis had done for the leper, he had done for Christ himself. Just as Christ had appeared to St. Martin as a beggar, he appeared to Francis as a leper. In a real sense, Francis began to perceive that each leper was a Christ and thus treated them accordingly. He began to visit them, care for them, and become their friend. Many years later, after the reception of the stigmata, Francis wanted to go back to the leprosaria where he had spent so many days.

Francis began to pray more and more. And not only did he pray in solitary places, he also prayed in churches. As he knelt before a crucifix in the decaying church of San Damiano just beneath the walls of Assisi, he heard Christ speak to him: "Francis, go and repair my church." Later, Francis understood that Christ means *the* Church; but at that moment at San

[2]From the beginning of Francis' "Testament," which he composed as he lay dying in 1226. This translation is from *Francis and Clare: The Complete Works* tr. Regis Armstrong and Ignatius Brady (Ramsey, NJ: Paulist Press, 1982), p. 154.

Damiano, his thoughts were of stone and mortar for poor San Damiano.[3]

Francis heard this call not from the image of a Christ who ruled the universe but from a Christ with nails in his hands and feet and a lance wound in his side. That Christ was quite like the leper, who was disfigured and the object of scorn and ridicule. Francis must have noted this relationship. It is important that Francis responded immediately to the call to rebuild the Church by giving the priest there all the money he had with him. His first response is still within the framework of the emerging values of the merchant class in Italy. In fact, he carried it beyond the bounds of legality when he sold some cloth belonging to his father and used that money for his renovation project at San Damiano.

There is another important aspect of Francis' response to Christ's call at San Damiano. It would have been easy and rational to take some time to think about precisely what Christ's words meant. It was not every day that Christ spoke to him, and in a previous vision, his first interpretation of what Christ had said proved to be quite wrongheaded.[4] Yet Francis responded as best he could in obedience to the words of Christ as he understood them at the moment. Francis never lost this instinct of beginning with what words clearly meant in a literal sense and allowing deeper meanings to emerge as he lived out their most obvious meaning. This is an important kind of faith—God tells us enough to get us started and he will aid us as we move in deeper ways to respond to His call. It is also an expression of humility—I will respond in obedience, which Benedict called the first step of humility.[5] It is a matter of trusting God's words more than one's

[3]II Cel 10 and *LM* II, 1. Early paintings of this story can be seen in Assisi and Siena. See also Edward Peters, "Restoring the Church and Restoring Churches: Event and Image in Franciscan Biography," *Franziskanische Studien* 68 (1986): 213-236.

[4]This is the story of the vision of arms. Francis saw a palace filled with weapons of war marked with the sign of the cross. He interpreted this vision to mean that he would be a successful knight. Bonaventure explains that, " . . . he had no experience in interpreting divine mysteries nor did he know how to pass through visible images to grasp the invisible truth beyond" (*LM* I, 6).

[5]"The first degree of humility is obedience without delay. This is the virtue of those who hold nothing dearer to them than Christ." See *St. Benedict's Rule for Monasteries* tr. Leonard Doyle (Collegeville, MN: The Liturgical Press, 1948), ch. 5.

own intellect or will. Later, Francis had a love for a simple friar named John who blinked when Francis blinked and coughed when Francis coughed (II Cel 190). It is not that Francis thought that this was all there was to being a follower of God. But it was an expression of trust and surrender. Perhaps this explains why Francis had some fear of books and intellectual activity. Scholars spend a good deal of their time explaining why words do not really mean what they appear to, and in Francis' time there was a lot of effort spent explaining obtuse allegorical meanings of a biblical text rather than acting on its literal message. Brother John was a welcome antidote to arid scholarship that led to intellectual pride rather than humble submission to God.

Until Francis used money from his father's business to rebuild San Damiano, Pietro took no drastic action against his son. No doubt, Pietro was angry with his son's dissatisfaction with all that he had worked hard to provide him with. He was probably hurt, perplexed, and angry. Did he think it was just a phase Francis would pass through on his way to bourgeois respectability, much as fathers hoped that long hair and peace buttons were temporary aberrations in the 1960s? But when Francis began to tap into his father's resources in order to support his craziness, something had to be done. He did not want to be regarded as a fool, and he did have two other sons who were more interested in the family business.[6]

Pietro asked the civil authorities to take action, but they backed down because Francis claimed to be a servant of God and outside their jurisdiction.[7] He probably did not have a very good legal argument for this position, but it was not an issue the city's leaders wished to pursue. Thus, Pietro turned to Bishop Guido, who summoned Francis.

Francis was bright enough and old enough to understand the issues in the case and to guess the outcome. But by this time, he understood enough to be willing to make a commitment to God

[6]Trexler thinks that Francis' brothers were the sons of Lady Pica by a previous husband, and that the legal complexities concerning Pietro's resources were great.

[7]The only source for this detail is *Legend of the Three Companions* 19. I believe that it deserves credibility.

that included breaking with his earthly family. In the time since he had given up his military career, he had had several experiences that had brought him joy. They included praying in lonely places, begging, kissing lepers, experiencing God's call to rebuild the Church, and working with his hands to fix up San Damiano. What was the common thread of these experiences? He had by this time begun to figure it out. In begging for alms at San Pietro in Rome, was he not like Christ and the apostles, who had no where to lay their heads? In embracing a leper, was he not embracing Christ and also imitating Him? When he prayed on the mountain, he was like Christ, who went into the wilderness to pray. And he was serving Christ in helping to rebuild his house, where He was present under the species of bread and wine. It was Christ who was at the center, Christ who was his source of joy. When he imitated Christ, he found joy. When he was treated as Christ was, with ridicule and scorn, he was entering into the experience of the utter humility of God, who took human form, lived in poverty, and died in agony. Christ was indeed in that leper. Christ had experienced rejection and even betrayal from those whom he had called to be his disciples.

The sources are clear that Francis did not plan to strip himself naked before the bishop in the presence of his father. Until now, he had kept a foot in each camp. He prayed and begged and repaired, but he still had the "insurance" of family and friends. He could still go back to being a carousing young man who would inherit the family business. To live with that sort of insurance was certainly not to imitate Christ, and it was the imitation of Christ that made him so happy in a way that bolts of cloth and drinking bouts never could. Grace was now active in Francis in such a way that he was prepared to make an irreversible commitment. This was not a youthful rebellion that spent itself before age 30; Francis was not testing others; Francis was not "making a statement" and then rejoining the establishment.

So naked he stood. Pietro was angry, probably because of his own powerlessness rather than specifically because of Francis' embarrassing rejection of him and what he stood for. Pietro wanted control over Francis; he had even locked him in the family's basement for a while, a perfectly legal act in a society where heads of families had certain kinds of authority that only governments have today. But his wife had let Francis go when he was away. Although he had expressed his anger to her upon his return, he must have known that cellar-dwelling was not changing Francis' mind. Perhaps Pietro thought he could get his son as well as his money back when he forced the issue.

As Francis stood naked that day, he showed no anger toward his father but instead stated his total allegiance to his heavenly Father. After the bishop temporarily covered Francis' nakedness with his cloak, he obtained for him a used tunic. According to Bonaventure, he then marked a cross on it (*LM* II, 4). Francis had "put on Christ" (cf. Eph 4:24; Col 3:12). He had "taken up his cross" (Lk 9:23). He was naked, born again to a life that imitated Christ's not only by virtue of being flesh and blood but by virtue of the grace to live a life like His.

According to II Celano, when Francis took off his clothes, he said that while previously he had spoken of his father Pietro Bernardone, now he could freely say, "Our Father, Who art in heaven." When one thinks seriously about the words of the Lord's Prayer, which Francis had no doubt recited hundreds of times, it is quite radical in its implications. It calls for the reign of God on earth by asking that God's will be done on earth just as it is in heaven. In both words and pictures, heaven was represented in the Middle Ages as a community that shared in all of God's graces. The prayer also asks only for this day's bread. Francis had been part of a system in which it was regarded as good to accumulate wealth, at least in part as "insurance" against future woes. Only with no wealth and therefore no insurance could Francis for the first time pray the Our Father seriously and without reservation. It is significant that Celano quotes Francis as saying that he can now *freely* recite this prayer. [8]

In the years preceding Francis' disrobing before the bishop, he had come to see the world in radically different terms from what

[8]Michael Crosby, a Franciscan, has written a valuable book about the Lord's prayer that is inspired by Francis' life and words. See *Thy Will Be Done: Praying the Our Father As Subversive Activity* (Maryknoll, NY: Orbis Books, 1977), esp. pp. 32-33.

he had previously understood. He began his transformation with a crisis caused in part by his imprisonment and illness. He had found a certain emptiness in a life focused on earthly fame and material possessions. However, he did not condemn the material possessions that others sought with such great zeal; that has been the mistake of so many people who have become disillusioned with a value system that placed material possessions at the center. Francis did not throw bolts of cloth in the river or drain the vats in which they were dyed. Francis saw the obstacle to joy and perfection not in his father's storerooms but within himself. Without articulating it, he discovered that it was his attitude toward worldly things that was the problem rather than the things themselves.[9]

Francis developed a radically new vision, one that inverted the values prevalent in the emerging bourgeois society of cities like Assisi. His vision was filled with paradoxes: poverty is true riches, weakness is strength, rejection is happiness. Once he realized the truth of these paradoxes, there was no room for compromise. If poverty is true wealth, then extreme poverty was the greatest riches.

Just as Francis' conversion is the result of grace perfecting nature, so too does his new vision use many of the constructs of the world he had grown up in. Francis remains a warrior, but one who is armed only with the cross. His armor, that old tunic, bore the coat of arms of his master—the sign of the cross. He remains a troubadour, but the songs he sang were about a love quite different than he imagined when he first learned the style. Courtesy remains a central virtue.

In the months that followed, he was a knight without an army. He sang in the woods, begged materials for San Damiano and then other churches including the Porziuncola. He was attacked by bandits in the woods. In Assisi, many mocked him, threw mud at him, called him a madman; one of his despisers was his brother. While Francis was still laboring at San Damiano, the priest there prepared special food for him because Francis had come from

[9]This is the distinction that Augustine finally learned to make in *Confessions* VII, 16.

affluent circumstances and was a picky eater. When Francis-realized this, he knew that this vestige of his old life must be severed. Thus, he went begging for scraps in the town with a bowl. He almost became ill as he sat down to eat the swill he had collected, but once again conquered himself and ate what was before him. It tasted wonderful. We can believe Francis and still not want the recipe. In order to understand this event, it is useful to think of how Augustine described some pears he stole as a youth:

> If any part of one of those pears passed my lips, it was the sin that gave it flavour.[10]

It was not the fruit itself that Augustine tasted; the good taste was from the sin of stealing, which had given him such great pleasure. The story of Francis and the bowl of slop is the other side of Augustine's coin. The food was good because of the virtue of poverty. Francis rejected the ways of the rich just as God did when he chose to enter the world in poverty. Obtaining his food as a poor man is another way of identifying with Christ, and it is from the virtue of his act that the good taste derived.

There were other events that occurred in these years that also had new meanings. Francis faced scorn and ridicule with joy. Had Christ not been scorned and ridiculed? He was treated as a madman. And he *was* by the standards he had grown up with. But this new madness was foolishness for Christ, as Paul called it (cf. 1 Cor 3:18-19). Once he was too bashful to beg from a group of men in Assisi, whom he probably knew; he returned when he realized his cowardice (II Cel 13).

Francis had at first adopted the dress of a hermit, with sandals and a leather belt. However, after hearing during mass the gospel text in which Christ told the apostles to take no money nor a belt nor sandals nor a staff with them (Mt 10:9), Francis rid himself of all these things and began to wear what would become his "uniform"—a tunic, a rope, and underwear.[11] When Francis

[10]*Confessions* tr. R.S. Pine-Coffin (New York: Penguin, 1961), II, 6.

[11]The only visual representation of this event is in a painting in the church of Santa Croce in Florence.

stripped himself naked, he did not completely realize the implications or dimensions of poverty. Certainly, he did not consider what it meant in legal terms. Poverty was having no money and no "insurance". When he rid himself of his sandals and belt, he defined for himself the most radical poverty possible. If he could have gone completely naked, he probably would have. Given that impossibility, he wanted as little as possible. If Christ died naked on the cross, then Francis' life of imitation had to involve being as close to naked as possible.

It is also important to recognize that the gospel text that Francis heeded that day was specifically directed to the apostles who were being sent out to preach the good news. Francis was beginning to perceive his own call to apostleship. Had not apostles left their families and rid themselves of all but the barest necessities? But if Francis is to become an apostle, what does that mean in a positive sense? What exactly is the call to apostleship? There is no simple answer, for we find the apostles doing quite a few different things in the gospels, Acts, and the New Testament letters. However, it is clear that one central element, made even more emphatic in the medieval legends of the apostles, was the proclamation of the good news. At this point in Francis' life, however, he was not yet ready to preach:

> As yet Francis did not preach sermons to the people [he] met; nevertheless in passing through towns and castles he exhorted all men and women to fear God and to do penance for their sins. . . .[12]

Francis knew that preaching is done first by example and then by precept (I Cel 36), as Gregory the Great had written centuries before in the *Pastoral Care*.[13] Yet, in exhorting people to do penance, he was in a sense preaching, for that was always the chief element in his proclamation of the good news. And for Francis, that is the best possible news—that one can sin but that God is

[12]*Legend of the Three Companions* 33.

[13]Tr. Henry Davis, *Ancient Christian Writers*, #11 (New York: Newman Press, rpt. 1978), II, 3.

merciful to all who turn to him. The evidence is that he allowed His own son to die naked on the cross in order to reconcile sinners to Him.

As Francis continued to repair churches, beg for materials, live in destitute poverty, and endure hardship and ridicule, he began to attract followers. Within a relatively short period of time, he was joined by several other people from Assisi including a wealthy man, a priest, and a simple man. The brotherhood was born. They had witnessed Francis' transformation and knew of his rejection of his family and material goods. I doubt that it was Francis' stripping himself naked or his quixotic repairing of collapsing churches that attracted these men. It was his joy. It was that his radical reversal of traditional standards of behavior had produced a joy that had eluded Francis and them. They saw that grace does transform nature. They did not look forward to eating slop for its own sake, but they desired the joy that Francis had found in that act. It may have seemed crazy to them, but Francis had discovered something that few others knew. He possessed something that few others possessed. Bonaventure could only describe it in the language of paradox: "What a priceless treasure poverty is" (*LM* IV, 7)!

Francis did not quite know what to do when first Bernard of Quintavalle and then Peter Catani joined him in this harsh life. According to the *Legend of the Three Companions*, they decided to consult those portions of scripture in which Christ spoke of renouncing the world. When they found a copy of scripture, however, they had no idea how to find the passages they were seeking.[14] So they prayed and opened the book three times. In a real sense, the earliest form of a rule of life was the three passages they found: the command to sell all and give to the poor (Mt 19:21), the exhortation of Christ to the apostles to take nothing with them on their journey (Mt 10:9; Lk 9:3), and the call to self-denial (Mt 16:24). Francis had studied scripture very little, but he believed that prayer was a reliable means to discover its wisdom.

[14]*Legend of the Three Companions*, 28, 29.

This primitive brotherhood faced a number of problems. When the brothers approached a town, many were terrified by their appearance. Some thought they were mad and thus were fearful of them.[15] Others thought they were, "wild men of the woods."[16] They were even feared as thieves, although certainly not accomplished ones. Some might have feared that they were heretics. It is easy for us to think that Francis and his earliest followers would have been perceived as holy men, even if a bit eccentric and fanatical. Instead, people played jokes on them. Sometimes children stole their garments (presumably when they were bathing or sleeping) and left them naked. People threw mud at them and held on to their cowls when they were trying to walk. Jesters put dice in their hands.[17] How little did the tormentors understand! In their actions, they gave Francis and his followers the opportunity to experience what Christ had experienced in the events leading up to the crucifixion. Paul writes in Romans in his discussion of baptism that one must die with Christ in order to rise with Christ (Rom 6:1ff). For Francis, this defined how he lived his life. In his sharing in Christ's passion, he was preparing to share in his triumph over death. But even Francis could not have imagined that, for him, sharing Christ's passion would ultimately involve receiving Christ's wounds.

Despite cruelty and violence, Francis always greeted people with, "The Lord give you peace" (I Cel 24). It is obvious that Francis meant much more by these words than simply calling for an end to physical violence. He is asking for that peace which the world cannot give. Nevertheless, Francis was an apostle of peace in the sense of wanting to end war and violence. It is in these early years that Francis' commitment to peace was established. It would become more profound after he witnessed bloodshed in the crusades in 1219 when he was in the Middle East. Yet the essential commitment comes at this time. There are stories of Francis bringing an end to civic violence in Arezzo, Bologna,

[15]*Legend of the Three Companions*, 34.

[16]*Legend of the Three Companions*, 37.

[17]*Legend of the Three Companions*, 40.

Siena, and Assisi in the various Franciscan legends. The genesis of Francis the peacemaker is in these early years after his conversion.[18]

Once again there is a paradox, however. Francis continues to think of himself as a warrior and his order as an army. He calls his brothers knights and refers to himself as the herald of the king (*LM* II, 5). All of the military language has been transformed by grace. The warrior who fights for things of the world is an agent of death. But those who do battle against sin are warriors who bring peace. Francis has transformed troubadour love songs into love songs to God. He uses the language of courtly love to describe his bride, Lady Poverty. In worldly language, knights work to kill others just as poverty is debilitating and vile. From this new perspective, true knights seek to destroy sin and thus are preservers and enhancers of life.

In the early years of the brotherhood, Francis and his followers practiced extreme acts of asceticism:

> For when they wanted to give themselves to prayer, they made use of certain means lest sleep should take hold of them; some were held erect by hanging ropes lest their prayers should be disturbed by sleep stealing over them; others put instruments of iron about their bodies, and others wore wooden girdles of penance. If, as it can happen, their sobriety were disturbed by an abundance of food or drink, or if because they were tired from a journey, they surpassed even a little the bounds of necessity, they mortified themselves very sharply by an abstinence of many days. Lastly, they tried to repress the promptings of the flesh with such great mortification that often they did not refrain from stripping themselves naked in the coldest weather and from piercing their bodies all over with the points of thorns, even to causing the blood to flow (I Cel 40).

I quoted such a long passage precisely because it seems on the surface so severe and distasteful to the modern reader. Many

[18]See my "Beatus Pacificus: Francis of Assisi as Peacemaker," *The Cord* 33 (1983): 130-136.

modern versions of Francis' life, especially those for a wide audience, ignore this severe asceticism. There is even more to it than what is quoted above. Francis often mixed his food with ashes and fasted to an extreme that seems impossible to modern people living in the West. Francis practiced flagellation on occasion and referred to his body as Brother Ass. Many people view the kind of asceticism Francis practiced as more than excessive zeal, almost as heresy. Since God created the body, it must be good; it was the heretical Cathars who argued that the flesh is evil. However, the issue is not this simple. For Francis, imitation of and ultimately union with Christ is or should be the goal of every person. No one was ever more singleminded than Francis of Assisi. Whatever moves a person toward that goal is good. For Francis, nothing does that more than poverty. Any impediment that occurs on the journey toward God must be avoided. Since cares about earthly things such as food, drink, clothing, or sex are impediments, our appetites for such things must be curbed.

Ascetic practices are the disciplining of the body; if eating or desiring fancy food leads to thoughts of what is necessary to obtain delicacies, the person is diverted from his spiritual journey. If the body is punished or disciplined when its wants divert attention from the soul's journey to God, it will be less inclined to long for those things in the future. Once after rolling naked in the snow in response to a lustful thought, Francis never felt the flame of passion again (LM V, 4). In that same story, we learn that Francis recognized the consequences of surrendering to sexual temptation—having wife and family. Francis did not condemn marriage or the procreation of children. But his way to Christ was through absolute poverty and concentration on imitating Christ as literally as possible. If he had a family, he would have the responsibility to feed and clothe it; and that would divert him from his journey. I often recall a conversation I once had with a Trappist monk. I expressed my admiration for him living in poverty and austerity and for the hours each day he spent in prayer. How strong he must be, I suggested. He responded that he was living the monastic life because of his weakness; the strong are those who take care of their families and work in the world and are still able to make the journey toward God despite their involvement. I am not sure Francis would quite say this, but it is important to remember that he loved and respected all sorts and conditions of humans. He never condemned the wealthy, nor did he refuse their generosity or hospitality. He even established the Third Order for those who did have families and property. But his path could contain no diversions or even resting places.[19]

Francis' life was also not just a personal journey to God. It was the prophetic life that showed others the journey in its purest form. This is the point Bonaventure makes when he tells a story of one of Francis' most bizarre penitential acts. During an illness, he ate a little meat and afterwards decided to repent of his gluttony:

> After [entering the town of Assisi], he entered the principal church in procession with the friars whom he had brought with him, and there he took off his habit and put a rope around his neck. Then he told one of the friars to lead him to the stone where criminals were punished, in full view of all the people. . . . His action certainly seems to have been intended rather as an omen reminiscent of the prophet Isaiah than as an example. However, it is a lesson in true humility and shows the true follower of Christ that he is bound to disregard all earthly praise and subdue the displays of bloated pride, while renouncing all lying pretense (*LM* VI, 2).

Although it is important to treat Francis' life as the story of a particular individual, it is also necessary to consider its prophetic quality. Old Testament prophets sometimes did bizarre things (Ezekiel in particular), lived ascetic lives (Elijah), and in general spoke and acted in ways that set them off radically from prevailing values and norms. So too with John the Baptist, the New Testament prophet whom both Thomas of Celano (II Cel 3) and Bonaventure (*LM* Prologue, 1) liken Francis to. Although Francis

[19]I treasure the insights I have gained by my opportunities to spend time in several Trappist monasteries, especially the Abbey of the Genesee, right across the Genesee valley from my university.

was not fully aware of the prophetic dimension of his life in his early years, others such as Bonaventure have perceived it in looking back on the events and words of his life.

In 1209, this early phase of Francis' life ended when he and his eleven brothers went to Rome and received papal approval for their brotherhood.

The years around the moment of Francis' disrobing before Bishop Guido of Assisi saw Francis change from one sort of carefree life to another. In his youth he had not worried about the "bottom line" of the cloth business and spent much time and money enjoying good food and song in the company of his friends. Although he dreamed of military success, it is not clear from the evidence that he ever prepared for a military career with the long hours of practicing skills that a successful warrior needed. He soon turned to a radically different carefree life. He was not concerned with earthly honors or fame and rejected pleasures of the moment and satisfaction of the body's appetites for a life of abject poverty and the desire to experience what Christ had experienced on earth and to do the work Christ called his apostles to do. He was more carefree in this new life than in the old. There were no parties or banquets to plan. He had the freedom of giving no thought about tomorrow because he trusted God, who provided all of his creatures with necessities. There was a group of men who looked to Francis the way his fellow revellers had, but he insisted that as a brotherhood they all rely on God rather than their relying on him.

By 1209, all the basic elements of Francis' spirituality were present in him. The rest of his life would in a sense be the experience of the implications of these things.

3

Saint Francis and the Physical World

Most High, all-powerful, good Lord,
Yours are the praises, the glory, the honor, and all blessing.
To You alone, Most High, do they belong,
and no man is worthy to mention Your name.
Praised be You, my Lord, with all your creatures,
especially Sir Brother Sun,
Who is the day and through whom You give us light.
And he is beautiful and radiant with great splendor,
and bears a likeness of You, Most High One.
Praised be You, my Lord, through Sister Moon and the stars,
in heaven you formed them clear and precious and beautiful.
Praised be You, my Lord, through Brother Wind,
and through the air, cloudy and serene, and every kind of weather
through which You give sustenance to Your creatures.
Praised be You, my Lord, through Brother Fire,
through whom You light the night
and he is beautiful and playful and robust and strong.
Praised be You, my Lord, through our Sister Mother Earth,
who sustains and governs us,
and produces varied fruits and colored flowers and herbs.[1]

[1] *Francis and Clare: The Complete Works* tr. Regis Armstrong and Ignatius Brady (Ramsey, NJ: Paulist Press, 1982), pp. 38-39. Francis wrote this part of the "Canticle" while staying with the Clares at San Damiano. Later, he wrote two other verses of the song; here, I have presented only the part he wrote at San Damiano.

In the twentieth century, Francis is probably better known for his love of nature than for any other single element of his life. Popes have named him as the patron saint of animal protection societies and of ecology. Countless statues and windows show him with birds or the wolf of Gubbio. Lynn White has argued that Francis initiates a new way for Christians to understand the created world.[2] A popular book of the seventies described Francis in the title as a nature mystic.[3] An English friar has even "updated" Francis' famous "Canticle of the Creatures" so that it includes Brother DNA and Sister Nuclear Fusion.[4]

When Francis declared that his father was "Our Father Who art in heaven" as he stripped himself naked before the bishop of Assisi, he certainly did not realize all the implications of that pronouncement. If God is the father of all human beings and indeed of all things that are, then all God's creatures are related by virtue of having the same father—i.e., they are brothers and sisters. Thus, Francis came to understand that God's family included crickets and rocks and sticks as well as fellow humans of all sorts and conditions. Exactly how Francis came to this insight is not clearly spelled out in the surviving documents. The seeds of this view of the universe can be found in the opening chapters of Genesis, and Francis was intimately acquainted with scripture and one of its brilliant interpreters. When Francis walked through the woods or listened to a bird chirp, it was not just an encounter between him and another creature; it was an encounter always mediated by what Francis understood about God and nature as related in scripture.

Francis was not particularly interested in crickets or rocks *per se*, but rather because they represented moral qualities and teachings, and they also helped lead Francis to a greater understanding and experience of the Father he shared with them. Francis was not particularly interested in an animal's behavior or

[2]"The Historical Roots of Our Ecologic Crisis," *Science Magazine*, March 19, 1967.

[3]Edward Armstrong, *Saint Francis: Nature Mystic* (Berkeley: University of California Press, 1973).

[4]Eric Doyle, *St. Francis and the Song of Brotherhood* (New York: Seabury, 1981), pp. 188-189.

an inanimate object's properties for their own sakes. Instead, he found in nature answers about or at least clues to the nature of the Creator and an understanding of His laws. We will need to explore Francis' approach to and his insights from nature in some detail. The best place to begin is with Bonaventure's words:

> Aroused by all things to the love of God, he rejoiced in all the works of the Lord's hand and from these joy-producing manifestations he rose to their life-giving principle and cause. In beautiful things he saw Beauty itself and through his vestiges imprinted on creation he followed his Beloved everywhere, making from all things a ladder by which he could climb up and embrace him who is utterly desirable. With a feeling of unprecedented devotion he savored in each and every creature—as in so many rivulets—that Goodness which is their fountain-source. And he perceived a heavenly harmony in the consonance of powers and activities God has given them, and like the prophet David sweetly exhorted them to praise the Lord (*LM* IX, 1).

When Francis referred to *Brother* wolf or *Sister* water, he was not just using a clever rhetorical strategy. He meant those titles quite literally. The implications are quite extraordinary for one who takes this brotherhood seriously. What is the proper way to treat a brother or sister? Brothers and sisters are not to be exploited or manipulated; they are loved and respected because of the intimate link between siblings based on their common ancestry. To expand this concept to include everything that exists and to do it seriously leads to some rather startling behavior on Francis' part. In one instance, one of his garments caught on fire, but he refused to put it out because he did not want to harm Brother Fire.[5] Similarly, we are told that Francis did not like to extinguish a candle or lamp. He set loose fish that had been caught, picked worms up off the road, and seriously preached to flowers (I Cel 80-81). These are among Francis' most bizarre

[5] *Legend of Perugia* 49.

"eccentricities" from a modern viewpoint. But what we really see here is a man who takes absolutely seriously his belief in the brotherhood of creatures and the fatherhood of God and tries to act on that belief all the time. One is tempted to wonder whether Francis thought the flowers heard his sermons. That is not such a silly question as it is often made out to be. In one obvious sense, Francis realized that flowers do not possess the organs of hearing. However, he believed that it is the nature of all things to praise their creator.[6] Francis may not have had any idea how flowers or rocks would or could do such a thing, but he probably believed that they could. And his reminders to the flowers to praise their creator are not much different from a brother gently reminding a sibling of some important obligation.

Francis was no fair-weather friend and brother of the natural world. In the Canticle of the Creatures, he praises not just fair weather but also stormy weather and indeed all weather. One of the differences between Francis and many lovers of nature is that he rejoiced in all the natural world, not just its beautiful parts and moments. It is not particularly difficult for people to watch a wonderful sunset or gaze up at the stars on a clear night or stand on the rim of the Grand Canyon and have their thoughts elevated to things infinite and eternal. No doubt Francis had had such experiences as a young man; that is why it is so striking that there was a time in his life when, "the beauty of the fields, the pleasantness of the vineyards, and whatever else was beautiful to look upon, could stir in him no delight" (I Cel 3). And living in as beautiful a place in Umbria and on the slope of Monte Subasio as Francis did, he seems to have had a headstart over many of the earth's inhabitants in viewing the beauty of the created world.

Several stories from the early biographies make clear that what separates Francis from those inspired by a stunning sunset is that Francis found beauty and significance in the less aesthetically pleasing aspects of the physical world. A worm signified Christ because in Psalm 22, David, ancestor and prefiguration of Christ, proclaimed, "I am a worm and no man." In a leper, Francis

[6]See Augustine, *Confessions* I, 1.

discovered the image of Christ because of the prophetic descriptions of Christ in the Suffering Servant Song of Isaiah. When Francis saw two sticks crossed on the ground, they led him to meditate on Christ and his cross (I Cel 45). While some of the meanings Francis found in nature seem a bit farfetched in a world dominated by a scientific approach to nature, we should take them seriously. One of Francis' greatest gifts to posterity is alerting Christians to the principle that God is manifest in each detail of the physical world to those who know how to "see" him. However, one does not see what is there if one does not look upon creation as a family. If we only see nature in terms of what it offers us (the number of kilowatt hours a dammed river could provide or the number of bushels of wheat an acre of land can produce or the economic feasibility of running day trips into the Grand Canyon), we will never find the traces of God there. Exploitation does not allow for the manifestation of God in nature. Only by loving it and enjoying it because it shares with us creaturehood can one see what was manifest to Francis in the world of nature.

As I pointed out in the introduction, the world of nature was much more frightening and menacing to people in the thirteenth century than it is today, at least in the industrialized countries. Although we are reminded of nature's power when there are hurricanes, tornadoes, volcanic eruptions, and so forth, we have learned to "tame" or neutralize the effects of the power of nature in many ways. We can easily light the night, live in warmth even in extremely cold climates, be protected from the rain by waterproof clothing, plow and harvest using machinery. It is hard to remember what an enemy nature often seemed in the thirteenth century, but it was much more similar to biblical texts recalling the rocky soil and the wild beasts than anything most people in the industrialized countries of the world experience today. In Francis' day, forests were scary places where menacing beasts lived; this is a far cry from the experiences of city dwellers today who spend their vacations camping in the national parks.There were often no paths, commissaries, guidebooks, marked trails, forest rangers, or Airstream trailers. It is vital that we recognize that Francis developed and expressed his view of the natural world in this kind of historical setting. His love of the forest is not that of either the

Boy Scouts or the Sierra Club, although I think he would have liked both of those groups.

Francis was not naive about nature. He was aware that the world of nature contained many acts of violence committed by creatures on other creatures. On occasion he expressed his revulsion of such violence. Francis was once staying at a monastery; while there, a pig attacked and killed a lamb. Francis recalled Christ's death at the hands of evil ones. Francis cursed the pig, which soon died; its carcass became stiff, and no other animal would touch it (II Cel 111). It seems "uncharacteristic" of Francis' to have cursed anything that God had created, and some scholars tend to ignore this story or to treat it as an exception to Francis' love of nature. However, Bonaventure chose to include this story in the *Legenda Maior* in a chapter about Francis' loving compassion (VIII, 6). Just as the evil men who betrayed and condemned Jesus were created by God but nevertheless deserved condemnation because of their rejection of God's love, so too does the sow deserve condemnation. In fact, Bonaventure adds the following moral to the end of the story of the sow that killed the lamb: "If cruelty in an animal led to such a terrible end, what will be the lot of evil men when the time of punishment comes eventually?" Francis' view of nature is not sentimental or romantic.

However, there is clearly an innocence in the relationship between Francis and many of the creatures he encountered which is rooted in biblical texts. First, Francis took seriously Christ's words that the kingdom of God is at hand, and often proclaimed these very words. But what exactly does it mean to proclaim the kingdom of God, and how does one look for evidence of its presence? One obvious way is to look to Old Testament texts that prophesy the coming of the kingdom. In Isaiah, the prophet looks to a day when a shoot shall spring from the root of Jesse:

> Then the wolf shall live with the sheep,
> and the leopard lie down with the kid;
> the calf and the young lion shall grow up together,
> and a little child shall lead them;
> the cow and the bear shall be friends,
> and their young shall lie down together.

> The lion shall eat straw like cattle;
> the infant shall play over the hole of the cobra,
> and the young child dance over the viper's nest (Isa 11:6-8).

Francis found in his relationship with nature evidence of the presence of the Kingdom, and its presence became clear to many by observing Francis and various creatures.

Francis as much as any man who has lived took an idea, discovered the implications of that idea, and rejoiced in taking both the idea and its consequences, however radical they were, absolutely seriously. Often when people discover radical implications in something they believe, they adjust their beliefs in such a way as to lessen the consequences for their lives; or they rationalize that the radical implications are not quite as radical as they appear. Francis never adjusted and never rationalized; indeed, he seems to have rejoiced in discovering the most extraordinary consequences of taking his beliefs seriously in his life.

Two stories of Francis and nature are so popular and well-known that they deserve special attention. The story of the sermon to the birds near Bevagna appears in many of the early lives of the saint, and a study of how it develops suggests the range of meanings this story takes on over time. In I Celano 58, Francis sees a group of doves, crows, and daws. That this is a mixture of nice birds and menacing birds is important. Francis wishes to address all of them because they are his brothers just as Francis praises all kinds of weather in the "Canticle of the Creatures." Francis reminds the birds of God's gifts to them—feathers, wings, the pure air for a home. The birds responded as best they could by making certain gestures. Francis then blessed the birds with the sign of the cross and dismissed them. The following story describes birds that became silent when Francis urged them to do so in order to speak to a crowd in Alviano, and Celano refers to this event as a miracle. We can therefore infer that the sermon at Bevagna, in which the birds listened and did not fly away until they received Francis' blessing, is also regarded as a miracle.

That the sermon to the birds was understood as a miracle in the years immediately following Francis' death is confirmed by the visual tradition. In the earliest painting of events from the life of

Central figure of St. Francis with six stories from his life and miracles taken from I Celano. The artist is Bonaventura Berlinghieri from Lucca; it was painted in 1235. The painting is on a side altar of the church of San Francesco in Pescia. The upper left scene is the stigmatization; beneath it is Francis' sermon to the birds. The other four scenes are posthumous miracles. In the lower left is the cure of a crippled girl. Upper right is the cure of cripples and lepers; right center is the cure of a cripple at a bath. In the lower right scene is an exorcism of demons.

The sermon to the birds from the panel by Bonaventura Berlinghieri in Pescia. Francis holds a book, making clear that he is following and preaching the gospel. He bears the stigmata in his hands and feet, although in a historical sense he had not yet received the wounds at the time he preached to the birds at Bevagna. The two other friars make traditional gestures of wonder, so that it is clear that we are looking at a miraculous occurrence.

Francis, a panel by the Luccan painter Bonaventura Berlinghieri executed in 1235 for the church of San Francesco in Pescia, the sermon to the birds and the stigmatization are presented along with four posthumous miracles. That the stigmatization was regarded as a miracle is clear from Elias' letter of 1226.[7] We can assume that all of these stories in the Pescia dossal were thought of as miracles. Why was this particular miracle selected for representation by Berlinghieri and quite a few other artists in the thirteenth century? First, it was a miracle related to the deeds of other saints. Not only were there stories of other saints' interactions with birds, but there were numerous stories of animals acting tamely in the presence of a saint.[8] St. Blaise received food from birds while living as a hermit, and they did not fly away until he blessed them. He also miraculously was responsible for a wolf returning a pig it had snatched to its owner.[9] Thus, the sermon to the birds was part of a tradition and helped to make clear that Francis was a saint, for he did what other holy men of God had done before. This nicely complements the "new miracle" of the stigmatization.

The sermon to the birds also complements the stigmatization in a second way. The stigmatization is a miracle in which Francis is the recipient of a supernatural act. On the other hand, the sermon to the birds is a miracle that Francis performs. Francis has the grace to receive a miracle from God as well as the grace to perform miracles for the benefit of his fellow creatures.

The fact that Francis preached to the birds obviously relates the event to the larger Franciscan vocation of preaching. It is, for example, no accident that in I Celano, the story of the sermon to the birds immediately follows Francis' sermon to the sultan. Thus, this story of Francis preaching to the birds can also stand for preaching specifically and apostolic work more generally as the vocation of the friars. Since the stigmatization illustrates the

[7]This letter is printed in the *Omnibus*, p. 1895. It is discussed in detail in chapter six.

[8]Armstrong, pp. 42-100.

[9]There is a splendid painting of this story from the life of St. Blaise in the Art Museum (Pinacoteca) in Siena by Sano di Pietro.

central theme of Franciscan spirituality, *compassio*—i.e., suffering with Christ—the two stories again can be seen as complementary. The principal activity and the focus of their prayer and contemplation are represented by the sermon to the birds and the stigmatization. The fact that they appear together so often in early paintings makes clear that the friars in Francis' own time wanted to emphasize the two characteristics of Francis' life that these stories embody.

Close attention to the gospels makes the connection between the sermon to the birds and the sermon to the sultan clear. Most people are familiar with Luke's version of Jesus' post-resurrection call to preach repentance to all nations (Lk 24:47). However, the operative text here is Mark's version of Jesus' commission of the apostles: "Go forth to every part of the world, and proclaim the Good News to the whole creation" (Mk 16:15). This broader commission explains both Francis' motivation for preaching to various sorts of creatures and Celano's juxtaposition of the sermon to the birds with the preaching to the sultan.

When Bonaventure recounts Francis' sermon to the birds, he does not describe particular species of birds. He emphasizes that Francis greeted the birds, "as if they understood" (*LM* XII, 3). After telling three other stories, Bonaventure presents the lesson in the group of stories by saying that since even creatures without reason submitted to the miraculous powers of Francis, "a person would certainly have to be really perverse and obstinate to refuse to listen to St. Francis' preaching" (*LM* XII, 6). Here it is not the exhortation to the birds that is really the focus of the story. Rather, this story is a sign to humans to pay attention to what Francis (and his followers) have to say since even creatures not endowed with reason recognized the authenticity of Francis' call. Bonaventure's transformation of Celano's account is within the Franciscan tradition in the sense that from looking at this encounter of Francis and the birds, people can be led to the word of God and thus to God himself.

The later version of the story in the *Fioretti* provides still another insight into this encounter between Francis and the feathery creatures. First, the assembly of birds was the largest and most diverse that had ever gathered in the area. After a somewhat longer version of Francis' sermon calling on the birds to praise their creator, they bowed their heads, indicating their understanding and pleasure at what Francis had said. As they flew away, they first sang and then dispersed in four straight lines—i.e., they made a cross in the sky. This suggested to the author both a sign of Francis' coming stigmata and a sign of the friars' mission to preach to the ends of the earth. In this version of the story, the themes found in both Celano and Bonaventure are brought together. It is a miracle story and one that illustrates Francis' relationship with his fellow creatures. However, the added elements in the *Fioretti* suggest the story's importance both as it points toward the stigmatization and to the Order's work in the world.[10]

The story of the wolf of Gubbio is not found in any of the early accounts of Francis' life, but only in the *Fioretti.*[11] The earliest visual representation of the story was painted in the last quarter of the fourteenth century.[12] Thus it does not rest on a firm historical foundation. However, the story is important for what it teaches about how Francis related to the natural world, and it is certainly a story filled with the spirit of Francis.

There was a wolf living near Gubbio that attacked and devoured both animals and humans. Francis, armed with the cross (cf. Eph 5:13ff), sought out the wolf. When he found it, he made the sign of the cross over it, and it lay at the saint's feet like a lamb, a clear reference to Isaiah 11. Francis saw not a ferocious beast but a creature of God, and the wolf's radical change of nature suggests Francis as the proclaimer of God's kingdom. Francis severly chastised the wolf and told him that he could justly be put to death; however, he wanted to bring about peace between it and the citizens of Gubbio. According to Ezekiel, God does not want a sinner to die but rather to turn from wickedness and live (Ezek 18:23). Francis arranged a pact between the

[10] *Fioretti* 24.

[11] *Fioretti* 21.

[12] It is a damaged fresco in the church of San Francesco in Pienza, a town in the southern part of Tuscany.

townspeople and the wolf which both parties ratified. Before the ratification, however, Francis reminded the people of Gubbio of their sins and the fact that they cared more about the safety of their bodies than the safety of their souls.

This peace treaty is central to the story. Francis had proclaimed peace wherever he had gone. He had also acted in various ways to bring civil peace in Arezzo, Assisi, Bologna, and Siena.[13] In those cities, Francis was healing strife among people. His activity at Gubbio was similar to his other peace missions. Peace for Francis involved not only bringing *people* into harmony and cooperation but all of creation. After all, the peaceable kingdom as described in various parts of Isaiah's prophecy involved not only men turning swords into ploughshares but also lions and lambs lying down together and children playing over the cobra's hole. The achievement of universal brotherhood depended as much on converting the wolf of Gubbio as it did settling factional strife in Arezzo or conflicts between ecclesiastical and secular officials in Assisi. It is worth noting too that while Francis healed the former strife through prayer and the latter by means of a song, he established a formal peace treaty between the wolf and the people of Gubbio. We might have expected just the opposite. We might have supposed that Francis would heal the disputes between rational creatures by means of a formal agreement and the conflict between people and a beast by means of direct prayer or a soothing song. It is always dangerous to assume that Francis would act according to worldly wisdom, for Francis fulfilled in every way St. Paul's image of the fool for Christ. He was always turning the world's standards on their heads.

The story of the wolf of Gubbio as narrated in the *Fioretti* is Franciscan to its very core. Primarily, it tells of the need for and reward of repentance. The wolf became just and loving; consequently, it was provided for by the citizens until its death. So too, those people who repent and make their peace with God can be assured of His care for all their needs throughout eternity.

[13]See my "Beatus Pacificus: Francis of Assisi as Peacemaker," *The Cord* 33 (1983): 130-136.

Furthermore, the event provided Francis with an opportunity to call the citizens of Gubbio to repentance by recalling their excessive concern for their bodies. The wolf can only kill their bodies, but sinful behavior poisons their souls.

I want to discuss a rather obscure story involving Francis and birds taken from the *Fioretti.*[14] On a hill just beyond the city walls of Siena called the Alberino, Francis encountered a boy taking some turtle doves to market. Francis asked the boy for the doves, for they represented pure and humble souls that had fallen into the hands of cruel men. Francis addressed the birds by asking how they let themselves be caught. Then he promised that he would provide nests for them where they can follow God's will by multiplying. Certainly, what Francis sees in the situation and in the turtle doves is similar to the way Francis saw the lambs he rescued. I had never paid much attention to this story until I recently sat in the lobby of Covenant House in New York. This is a home/shelter for abandoned and runaway children, especially those caught up in the pornography industry in midtown Manhattan; its founder is a Franciscan, Father Bruce Ritter.[15] Along with some awards, there is a plaque on the wall of Covenant House that contains this story of Francis and the turtle doves. Its presence in this context is the perfect example of how Francis' spiritual vision provides for others new ways of seeing. Francis' concern for the birds and his promise to care for them so that they can do God's will is the model for Father Ritter's work with teenagers in New York. The tradition is carried out as new implications of Francis' treatment of and concern for his fellow creatures are discovered.

Francis of Assisi's love and praise of nature go far beyond the beautiful sunset and are more comprehensive than a modern environmentalist's concerns. The creatures are loved both for their own sakes because they share their creaturehood with us and are therefore parts of our family, and for the way they can

[14]*Fioretti* 22.

[15]Covenant House publishes a pamphlet entitled "The Covenant Experience." It is available from Covenant House, P.O. Box 731, Times Square Station, 340 W. 42nd St., New York, NY 10108.

lead us to God. Bonaventure understands creation itself as a book that contains knowledge of God; humanity's capacity to "read" that book was severely impaired by the Fall. Thus God authored a second book, scripture, to aid people. In the sixteenth century, John Calvin referred to the Bible as spectacles through which humans, with their vision impaired, could read God's universe.[16] Francis, perhaps more than anyone who ever lived, could read the book of the universe. He too of course saw nature as mediated through the lenses of scripture, but, wearing those spectacles, Francis' vision was closer to 20/20 than that of anyone else.

[16] *The Institutes of the Christian Religion* ed. Tony Lane and Hilary Osborne (London: Hodder and Stoughton, abridged ed. 1986), pt. 2, ch. 6.

4

Books and Learning

When we look for wisdom and guidance from the great Christian thinkers of the past, we almost instinctively look first to the great scholars. Highly trained philosophers and theologians such as Augustine, Anselm, and Thomas Aquinas come to mind immediately. We tend to equate theology with learning or at least regard the latter as a prerequisite for the former. Of course Paul in the first letter to the Corinthians distinguishes between earthly and heavenly wisdom, and he considered himself to be a fool for Christ (1 Cor 1:20-23). Still, it is often difficult for modern people with academic degrees and affiliations to take seriously the ability to read and interpret scripture of someone with not a lot of formal education who did not write very grammatically. No doubt Francis' lack of scholarly achievement was a stumbling block to many in the Middle Ages as well. In the last years of his life, Francis and the life he prescribed were challenged within his Order by a growing number of educated friars who had little desire to live as Francis had lived in the years after his conversion and who were a bit put off by his concern about learning corrupting the Order (II Cel 195).

It is easy today to criticize men who joined the Friars Minor but who were critical of some of Francis' practices and his inflexibility on a number of issues. A lot of modern Franciscan scholarship has taken the position that any deviation from Francis' own practices and lifestyle was a deviation from the holy life he lived and prescribed for others through his example and

Rule. If Francis did not read books and study biblical commentaries, then why should those who were his followers? If Francis preached to birds and flowers, why did his followers spend so much time preparing to preach to the most highly educated and placed people in Europe? If Francis so faithfully lived out the gospel life without a lot of formal education, why did his followers flock to Paris and Oxford and so many other centers of learning?

In some ways, this was the view of Francis' earliest biographer, Thomas of Celano. The issue of the role of learning in the Order was not of much concern to him when he wrote his *Vita Prima* in 1228, but by the time he composed his second life of Francis almost twenty years later, learning had become an important issue. Celano's concern with what too much booklearning was doing to the Order is not without a certain irony, for Celano himself was a learned man whose Latin was quite eloquent. Although Celano probably entered the Order after completing his education, it remains curious that Celano was so fearful of educated friars. The irony is greater when one considers that the chief way that friars learned about the deeds and teachings of their founder was by reading Celano's two sophisticated lives of Francis.

Our task here is to try first to discover precisely what Francis' attitude toward learning was and then to discuss how subsequent generations of friars understood the importance of study in the context of the Franciscan vocation.

Francis learned to read and write as a boy, something we would expect for the son of a prosperous merchant. He studied Latin and later wrote letters and his Rule in that language, although he was by no means a master of Latin prose. The most recent English translators of Francis' writings lament that he uses, "long and run-on phrases, clauses, and thoughts as well as poor grammatical construction."[1] He no doubt read as well as heard

[1]Regis Armstrong and Ignatius Brady in the introduction to their translation of the writings of Francis in *Francis and Clare: The Complete Works* (Ramsey, NJ: Paulist Press, 1982), pp. 6-8.

scripture from the time he was a boy. He also wrote Italian, for his "Canticle of the Creatures" is one of the earliest Italian poems; however, he wrote in the Umbrian dialect rather than in Tuscan, the basis of modern Italian.

That Francis learned to search through scripture and find passages relating to specific issues is clear from the fact that the primitive rule which Innocent III approved in 1209 was little more than a collection of scriptural quotations Francis had made. However, the *Legend of the Three Companions* suggests that before his conversion, he knew very little about the Bible in a formal sense. When Francis went to the little church of San Nicola in Assisi with Brothers Bernard and Peter Catani to consult scripture about their way of life,

> . . . being simple men, they did not know how to find the passage in the Gospel telling of the renunciation of the world. Therefore, they besought God that he would show them his will the first time they opened the book.[2]

By the end of Francis' life, he had assimilated much of scripture to such an extent that he cited it (by paraphrase, not verbatim) often. In the document he wrote and gave to Brother Leo after his stigmatization, he cites in less than one modern printed page four psalms, I Thessalonians, and Numbers;[3] it is quite unlikely that he thumbed through a Bible while composing this piece.

Despite Francis' lack of formal theological and scriptural training, he is presented in II Celano as a masterful exegete of scripture. A Dominican theologian who was a doctor of theology came to Francis while he was in Siena to ask him about a particularly thorny passage from Ezekiel: "If thou proclaim not to the wicked man his wickedness, I will require his soul at thy hand" (paraphrase of Ezek 3:6). This text would seem to make it almost impossible for anyone to enter the kingdom of heaven because, as the Dominican said, "I know many who, to the best of my

[2] *Legend of the Three Companions* 28.

[3] Tr. in *Francis and Clare: The Complete Works*, pp. 99-100.

knowledge, are in the state of mortal sin, but I do not always proclaim their wickedness" (II Cel 103). This clearly disturbed the Dominican theologian; he was aware of his own failure to upbraid and warn everyone he knew who had seriously sinned, and he feared for his soul. When Francis protested that he was unlettered and not the right person to ask to interpret this passage, the Dominican urged him to help because his academic colleagues had not provided him with an acceptable exegesis. Francis responded that we reprove the wicked by the way we live our lives and by what we say every day. The Dominican found this explanation of Ezekiel to be the best he had heard, and he concluded that,

> ... the theology of this man, based upon purity of life and contemplation, is a soaring eagle; but our learning crawls on its belly on the ground" (II Cel 103).

Here, the Dominican recognizes that exegesis based on experience and contemplation is ultimately better than interpretation based on academic labor.

Although Francis was humble about his ability to interpret scripture, he would agree with the Dominican. To understand the gospel involves living the gospel life and calling to God for help rather than reading commentaries on scripture. This is a lesson that was sometimes lost on some of Francis' followers, even some who knew him personally.

Once when Francis was ill, a friar suggested that he have a text from the Old Testament prophecies read to him. He responded:

> It is good to read the testimonies of Scripture; it is good to seek the Lord our God in them. As for me, however, I have already made so much of Scripture my own that I have more than enough to meditate on and revolve in my mind. I need no more, son; I know Christ, the poor crucified one (II Cel 105).

Francis had read and listened to scripture and had not only memorized it but made it a part of himself in the sense that its principles were his only guide and inspiration. Ultimately, the message of scripture is rather simple. Understanding is not the great challenge of scripture—living according to its teachings is. Francis did not need one more passage read to him; what he needed was further internalizing of the central message of scripture in order to live better.

Francis occasionally said or did things that would suggest to some today that he was anti-intellectual. For example, he supposedly said that,

> My brothers, who are being led by curious craving after learning will find their hand empty on the day of retribution. I want them rather to be made strong in virtues, so that when the times of tribulation come, they will have the Lord with them in their distress. For tribulation will come such that books, useful for nothing, will be thrown out of windows and into cubby-holes" (II Cel 195).

Once when a brother asked to have a psalter, Francis offered him ashes instead (II Cel 195).

In the final analysis, these stories should not be interpreted to mean that Francis despised learning. In fact, in his *Testament*, Francis states that, "We should honor and venerate theologians."[4] He realized that booklearning is a means to an end, that end being to live the life prescribed in scripture as preparation for union with God in this life and in the life to come. The problem for Francis was that often learning was done for its own sake—that is, its purpose was often perceived to be or at least to appear learned and to receive the advantages and honors accorded to the learned. That was at the heart of what Jacopone da Todi, the great Franciscan poet, meant when he said that Paris (the most important center for the study of theology in Europe) had destroyed Assisi.[5] Certainly, anyone who has ever been associated with an academic institution has some understanding of how prevalent this attitude is. It is a problem in any discipline, but for

[4]In *Francis and Clare: The Complete Works*, p. 154.

[5]*The Lauds* tr. Serge and Elizabeth Hughes (Ramsey, NJ: Paulist Press, 1982), #31.

theologians, this attitude is a contradiction of the teachings of scripture. If there is any counsel that runs through both Old and New Testaments, it is that people achieve God's friendship through humility. Jesus states quite unequivocally that the humble shall be exalted and the proud shall be brought low (Lk 14:11). If a theologian takes pride in the fact that he has read more glosses on Jesus' words than anyone else, then he is living a life opposite that clearly demanded by Christ. Another facet of academic pride is believing that a person who has not studied scripture cannot understand it as well as one who has; in other words, it is easy to believe that booklearning is the only way to true understanding. Francis must have been aware of the temptations that scholars fall prey to. He must also have noticed that scholars often glossed over (literally) some of the most radical and demanding passages of scripture and developed interpretations that made some of these texts compatible with the comfort of the detached and scholarly life. As I have emphasized above, Francis perhaps more than anyone else in the history of Christianity embraced and was not embarrassed by the most radical gospel precepts. As he discovered just how radical the gospels were, he not only did not back away but ran to embrace them. If the gospel required loving a leper as a brother and embracing him whenever he saw him, then Francis embraced a leper. He did not look to a gloss for the purpose of finding out why he does not literally have to embrace a leper to follow Christ's commandments. He simply did what the gospel said to do. This fear of glosses that distort or water down is clear in Francis' testament, which he dictated on his deathbed. He wrote about how the Rule and the Testament were to be understood:

> And I through obedience strictly command all my brothers cleric and lay, not to place glosses on the Rule or on these words, saying: They are to be understood in this way. But as the Lord has granted me to speak and to write the Rule and these words simply and purely, so shall you understand them simply and without gloss, and observe them with [their] holy manner of working until the end.[6]

[6]*Ibid.*, p. 156.

Learning was not only a source of pride but also, as already suggested, an opportunity to divorce words from deeds. Francis feared that his followers would spend more time studying what Jesus said about being poor than in practicing poverty. For Francis, this was a serious perversion. One of the reasons that some friars thought study was so important was that they were preachers who had to know what they were preaching about. Francis' approach was different. According to the *Legend of the Three Companions*, Francis did not begin to preach for quite a while after his conversion.[7] This is not because Francis had not studied scripture sufficiently but because he had to become a gospel *practitioner* before he became a preacher. To preach repentance did not require knowledge of the glosses on passages of scripture calling people to repent; it required that the preacher himself be a penitent! As Bonaventure said, "Because he had first convinced himself by practice of what he persuaded others to do by his words, he did not fear reproof but preached the truth most confidently" (*LM* XII, 8).

While Celano worried about the role of books and learning in the Order, Bonaventure took a somewhat different approach. He realized the flaw in the arguments of those who would demand that friars literally observe all of Francis' practices. Not all friars had Francis' gift of intuiting scripture and living out its precepts. We have all found ourselves in the situation of having to work very hard to achieve something that others seem to do effortlessly. Many times a student will come to talk about a paper he/she worked very hard on and received a C for, and in doing so will mention that his/her roommate did the assignment the night before it was due and got a B+. Sometimes the only response I can give is that the roommate is more gifted. Similarly, I have watched my two older sons do high school mathematics. One "saw" how to do a problem right away while the other struggled, usually unsuccessfully, to find a way to solve it. Francis was the recipient of exceptional grace, as he himself was always aware; these gifts were not a source of pride because they were free and

[7] *Legend of the Three Companions* 33.

undeserved gifts from God rather than something that Francis merited. How do Francis' followers imitate his success in living the gospel life if they do not have Francis' gift of spiritual intuition? One answer was that they could study scripture, something essentially unnecessary for Francis. In order to understand Bonaventure's argument, we must first examine how he described Francis' understanding of scripture:

> His unwearied application to prayer along with his continual exercise of virtue had led the man of God to such serenity of mind that although he had no skill in Sacred Scripture acquired through study, his intellect, illumined by the brilliance of eternal light, probed the depths of Scripture with remarkable acumen. Free from all stain, his genius penetrated the hidden depths of the mysteries, and where the scholarship of the teacher stands outside, the affection of the lover entered within (*LM* XI, 1).

Francis was a lover rather than a scholar. Shortly after this passage, Bonaventure retells the story from II Celano of the Dominican who asked Francis for an interpretation of Ezekiel 3:6.

Between the text quoted above and the story of Francis and the Dominican theologian, Bonaventure lays out his interpretation of Francis' attitude toward scholarship *within the Franciscan Order*. Bonaventure attributes the following words to Francis:

> I am indeed pleased [that learned men accepted into the Order devote themselves to the study of Scripture], as long as they do not neglect application to prayer, after the example of Christ, of whom we read that he prayed more than he read (*LM* XI, 1).

Imitation of Christ is always Francis' concern, and Jesus was not a scholar. According to Bonaventure, Francis saw scholarship as leading to the good Christian life which in turn led to preaching the gospel to others. Thus, for Francis, scholarship was a means to experiencing the gospel life and a secondary means to preparing friars to go out and preach the word of God. It is no accident that the chapter of the *Legenda Maior* that deals with Francis' understanding of scripture also discusses his spirit of prophecy.

Bonaventure is aware of the extraordinary irony in the passage quoted above. He makes clear that in order to imitate Christ, one should pray more than one should read because Christ did so. However, how do we know that Christ prayed more than he read? The answer is clear—we *read* that it is so in the gospels. Learning to imitate Christ thus may well involve study, but the study must lead to a life in which study is subordinate to prayer.

For Bonaventure, Francis' life was itself a significant—perhaps the most significant—gloss on scripture. Thus, Francis was to be read like a gloss. This gloss on scripture was not like a scholarly commentary. For those privileged to know the saint, they could "read" him directly; for those not so fortunate, they would have to rely on a gloss of that gloss, which was Bonaventure's *Legenda Maior*. That Francis' life, his gloss on scripture, was authentic was obvious because it had God's seal of authenticity—the stigmata. God himself sealed this gloss with his own seal, Christ's wounds, so that others would know that his life was a uniquely authentic gloss on scripture, far more important than any written at a university. Still, that gloss could not be read directly but through the medium of a book written in the most sophisticated Latin prose by one of the most subtle thinkers of the thirteenth or any other century.

Bonaventure provides guidance for the authentic Franciscan life for those not endowed with Francis' spiritual gifts, which means virtually everyone, since Bonaventure believed that Francis was uniquely endowed. Learning was not a perfect solution to the problem of guiding the friars to live an authentically Franciscan life. First, knowledge learned from books was ultimately inferior to that learned experientially. Second, the accumulation of knowledge was a great temptation to pride and an opportunity to avoid living the gospel by substituting talking about it. Bonaventure realized the dangers of encouraging friars to study, but he also understood that without study, many would have no starting point for following the gospel; and consequently the greatest of all scriptural glosses, Francis' own life, would not be passed on to future generations.

5

Action and Contemplation

Many medieval authors wrote about the relationship between the active and the contemplative life. Some used Mary and Martha from John's gospel to represent the contemplative and active lives; Dante used the Old Testament figures of Rachel and Leah.[1] In general, medieval discussions of the active and contemplative lives stressed the superiority of the latter. This conclusion is deeply rooted in both neoplatonic thought absorbed into Christianity and also the monastic tradition that had begun in the Egyptian desert in the third century. Some scholars have suggested that a major shift in western consciousness came in the Renaissance with the emphasis on the active life rather than the contemplative. I believe that this scheme comes out of a misunderstanding of both the Middle Ages and the Renaissance, but this is not the place to present a critique of the periodization of Western civilization. However, some brief comments will serve as introduction to Francis' contribution to the dialogue about the active and contemplative lives. First, it is probably wrong to view the issue as active versus contemplative as if somehow the two patterns of life were competitors. Instead, it makes more sense to view medieval texts on the subject as discussions of the proper relationship between active and contemplative dimensions of life.[2] No one could be completely contemplative although perhaps

[1] *Purgatorio* XXVII.

[2] I encountered this idea for the first time in a lecture by Professor Giles Constable, now of the Institute for Advanced Study at Princeton.

some of the orders of hermits that had *conversi* to provide for the needs of the hermits, for example the Carthusians and Camaldolese, came closest. On the other hand, a life without a contemplative dimension would have been seen as an aberration. A second preliminary thought about this issue is that if a significant change occurred in Christendom about the relationship between active and contemplative dimensions of life, it is probably to be traced to Francis of Assisi as much as to Renaissance humanists.[3]

The tension between the active and contemplative lives is evident in Francis even before his renunciation of goods in the presence of his father and the bishop of Assisi. Francis would go into the woods to pray alone but also rebuilt crumbling churches. Clearly, Francis was pulled toward both active and contemplative forms of life in the years between his conversion and the approval of his primitive rule by Innocent III. As he ministered to lepers and began to preach, he also continued to withdraw for prayer as well as to borrow the liturgical prayer of the older monastic orders.

According to Thomas of Celano, Francis and his followers openly discussed the question of the emphasis of the life of their Order as they returned to Assisi from Rome after receiving Innocent III's approbation. The question was put in terms of whether the friars should dwell among men or seek out solitary places. After praying, Francis, "chose not to live for himself alone, but for him who died for all, knowing that he was sent for this that he might win for God the souls the devil was trying to snatch away" (I Cel 35).

[3]The development of what is called civic humanism in Italy, especially Florence, at the beginning of the fifteenth century is significant in the development of western civilization; and I do not wish to suggest otherwise. However, later in that century, there was a great deal of emphasis on the contemplative life expressed by a number of great Renaissance thinkers including Pico and Baldassare Castiglione. Furthermore, the writings of Bernard of Clairvaux were among the most widely printed books in the second half of the fifteenth century in Italy; and that in itself warns us against assuming that the Middle Ages and Renaissance are easily distinguishable periods of history. For a discussion of the popularity of Bernard of Clairvaux's works in the fifteenth century, see Constable, "The Popularity of Twelfth Century Spiritual Writers in the Late Middle Ages" in *Renaissance Studies in Honor of Hans Baron* ed. Anthony Molho and John Tedeschi (Florence: Sansoni, 1971), pp. 3-28, esp. pp. 12-13.

Despite this conscious decision that Celano says occurred in the earliest days of the Order's history, the question of the relationship between action and contemplation for Francis and his friars would be raised again in several different contexts. Francis himself often withdrew from preaching and other apostolic ministries in order to be alone in prayer, and these periods of contemplation and prayer became longer and more frequent toward the end of his life.

The Church had great stories of both active and contemplative saints. On the one hand, there were the apostles, who spent their time preaching and ministering; but there were also great ascetic saints who lived either alone or in communities separated from the world. Francis knew both of these traditions well. Although he borrowed heavily from monastic thought and spirituality and lived for a while clad in hermit's dress, Francis realized early on that he did not want to be a member of an existing monastic order or to found another monastic order. When Francis was in Rome to meet with Innocent III, Cardinal John of St. Paul developed a real affection for the young man from Assisi and counselled him to become a cloistered monk or a hermit. In a rather blunt description of how Francis responded to this prince of the Church, Celano tells us that Francis refused his counsel because he had a, "pious leaning toward another life" (I Cel 33). This conversation was the immediate prelude to Francis' meeting with the pope. The saint was apparently rather consistent in his insistence that the friars were not to become another monastic order. According to the *Legend of Perugia*, some brothers approached Cardinal Ugolino, the Order's protector, to urge Francis to modify some aspects of the way of life he prescribed for the friars by appealing to the writings of Benedict, Augustine, and Bernard of Clairvaux. Francis responded to this request by saying that he did not want to hear any mention of the rules of these great saints because God had called him to be a "new fool."[4] Francis was not condemning the Benedictines, Cistercians, and Augustinian canons, but rather reminding the friars that their

[4] *Legend of Perugia* 114.

vocation was not that of the members of those orders. In an allegorical work entitled "Francis and His Lady Poverty" or "Sacrum Commercium," written perhaps as early as 1227, Lady Poverty asked Francis to show her his cloister. He took her to the top of a hill and showed her the whole world and said to her: "This, Lady, is our cloister."[5] This statement summarizes well what is both traditional and new for Francis. The idea of having a cloister, the enclosed space where the monastic community both labored and meditated, is still important to Francis; however, he has enlarged the community and thus the cloister to include all of humanity, indeed, all creation.

If Francis was not personally attracted to the stability of monastic life, he did recognize that living apart from the world for the purpose of prayer and contemplation was important and consistent with his conception of the Order of Friars Minor. A Spaniard reported to Francis that friars in his country lived in poor hermitages and that they alternated between periods of contemplation and periods of service to the other brothers. Francis was beside himself with joy when he heard stories about these Spanish friars (II Cel 178). Francis wrote a rule for Franciscan hermitages, perhaps based on what he heard of the Spanish brothers.[6] It includes the alternating of contemplation and service. The image of Mary and Martha is present in Francis' rule for hermitages,[7] and he refers to those serving the contemplatives as mothers and the contemplatives themselves as sons. It is clear that this rule is not for all friars but only for those who chose to live apart at least for a while.

Bonaventure presents a long discussion of Francis' internal struggle concerning whether he should live apart from society or preach. This portion of the *Legenda Maior* reads more like an article of Thomas Aquinas' *Summa* than a meditation of Francis. I suspect that what Bonaventure did here was to collect various

[5]Printed in the *Omnibus*, p. 1593.

[6]*Francis and Clare: The Complete Works* tr. Regis Armstrong and Ignatius Brady (Ramsey, NJ: Paulist Press, 1982), pp. 147-148.

[7]*Ibid.*, p. 147.

fragments concerning the issue of the active and contemplative lives and to assemble them in a form useful to the more educated friars of his own day. Bonaventure began with the question Francis asked his brothers: "What do you think, brothers, what do you judge better? That I should spend my time in prayer or that I should go about preaching" (*LM* XII, 1)? Francis first musters all the evidence in support of the contemplative life. He is a simple and unskilled preacher who has a greater gift of prayer than of teaching. Prayer is an accumulation of graces. Prayer leads to mystical union with God while preaching is distracting, and it dirties spiritual feet. In prayer, one addresses God, listens to his answers, and dwells with the angels, while preaching demands adaptation to human things. These are persuasive arguments of a kind often used in monastic literature to argue for the superiority of the contemplative life.

However, there is a powerful counter-argument that outweighs them all,

> . . . namely that the only begotten Son of God, who is the highest wisdom, came down from the bosom of the Father for the sake of souls in order to instruct the world with his example and to speak the word of salvation to men . . . (*LM* XII, 1).

Like every other decision Francis had to make, the key is the example of Christ. Although Christ went up into the mountains to pray (Lk 6:12), he spent most of his years of public ministry with people, teaching by word and example. Thus, Francis' decision about how he was to live his life is a foregone conclusion:

> And because we should do everything according to the pattern shown to us in him as on the heights of the mountain, it seems more pleasing to God that I interrupt my quiet and go out to labor (*LM* XII, 1).

Bonaventure tells us that even after Francis thought out the *sic et non* of the contemplative life, he still had doubts. Given the powerful words quoted just above, Bonaventure seems to be telling us that this was a serious dilemma that concerned the saint. According to the *Legenda Maior*, Francis sent brothers to solicit the opinions of Brother Silvester and of Clare on this matter. When he learned that both agreed that Francis should preach as a herald of Christ, Francis finally and unhesitatingly set out to preach.

The place of this series of passages from Bonaventure is important for understanding what he is telling us. It is the beginning of the chapter concerning his preaching and is immediately followed by the story of the sermon to the birds. At the end of this chapter, Bonaventure talks of Francis' mission to preach confirmed first by the pope and later by God himself in the imprinting of Christ's wounds on Francis' body.

The following chapter of the *Legenda Maior* is the story of the stigmatization, the culmination of Francis' life, which occurred while Francis was spending forty days on the solitary mountain of LaVerna in contemplation. Thus, Bonaventure has to consider still again the relationship of active and contemplative elements in the life of Francis. He begins with the image of Jacob's ladder with angels ascending and descending; he likens the movements of the angels to Francis' life, for he was either ascending to God through prayer and contemplation or descending in order to serve his neighbor:

> Therefore when in his compassion he had worked for the salvation of others, he would then leave behind the restlessness of the crowds and seek out hidden places of quiet and solitude, where he could spend his time more freely with the Lord and cleanse himself of any dust that might have adhered to him from his involvement with men (*LM* XIII, 1).

This passage is perhaps the final synthesis of action and contemplation in the life of Francis of Assisi. The active and contemplative lives are not two lifestyles that one must choose from. They are intimately related parts of the life of a Christian. One must step back from earthly involvements lest they lead one to forget the source of all things and the purpose of all things. It is an experience both to cleanse and to enjoy God. This time of prayer and contemplation prepares one to re-enter the world and seek its salvation. Contemplation without action can be self-serving, and action without contemplation soon loses sight of God's plan.

This great lesson of Francis, though often forgotten, is a source for the spiritual life of many working in the world today. Mother Teresa and her Order minister to the poorest of the poor in India and other places; however, she recognizes that prayer is the foundation of her apostolic ministry. Similarly, the Franciscan Bruce Ritter, founder of Covenant House, a shelter for runaway and abandoned youths in Midtown Manhattan, prescribes three hours of prayer—communal and individual—for members of the covenant community. He writes that, "Prayer is Community's first priority, for prayer supports and sustains our work with these kids."[8] These modern apostles recognize that there is a difference between ministry and social work, although the former borrows greatly from the latter. Apostolic work is the proclamation of the kingdom of God and of hope for all people; ministry is about working so that God's kingdom will come into being on earth, as it is in heaven. Living among lepers in Assisi or the outcasts of Calcutta or teenage prostitutes in New York is more than providing for their immediate needs, although it is that as well. It is proclaiming God's word where it appears to be most conspicuously silent. One cannot do that without the spiritual refreshment of prayer. One needs to be silent and alone in God's presence in order to bring together the things of heaven and earth. Francis could find joy in the simplest or most disgusting of things because he took the time to see the world through the eyes of the Creator rather than only through those of his fellow humans. Francis was no more a social worker in the modern sense than he was a naturalist. He was a man of God who lived from time to time in solitude in order to discover how the eternal invaded time, how the spiritual penetrated the material, how God's plan was discernible everywhere he looked. Action led Francis to con-

[8]From the pamphlet that Covenant House publishes entitled "The Covenant Experience."

templation, and in contemplation was revealed to him his call to action. Francis the apostolic man and Francis the mystic were not two sides or phases; they were fused. This becomes clearest when Francis in contemplation received the wounds of Christ, the man who ministered to all the world as he was nailed to the cross.

6

The Christmas Crib at Greccio

For the Christmas of 1223, Francis was at the little hermitage of Greccio in southern Umbria. It was on this occasion and at this remote place that Francis staged one of his most dramatic and significant acts. Christmas was a special feast for Francis because it was the celebration of God-become-man. Francis' whole spirituality was centered on living a life in conformity with that of Christ; thus, the celebration of the birth of the Savior was in some real sense the starting point of Francis' spiritual journey. For Francis, it was the poverty and humility of the nativity of Christ that set the tone of Jesus' entire ministry. He lived without wealth and without earthly comforts from his birth, and clearly this was God's own choice. Thus, poverty was Christ's constant companion from his first night on earth in an animal-feeding trough until his death upon the cross.

Of course, all the elements described above are either explicit or implicit in the gospel accounts familiar to all Christians in Francis' time as well as our own. And the Christmas liturgy is certainly one of the most beautiful of the liturgical year. Yet for Francis, the traditional liturgical celebration failed to awaken and illuminate many of those who heard it. One of Francis' and the friars' most difficult problems in the renewal of the Church was that the people they were addressing were already Christians. They knew the basic stories and teaching and had seen numerous visual images of familiar stories such as the nativity. How does one preach the word of God to those who think that they already understand it?

Francis decided that a more literal experience of the nativity was called for. He arranged for there to be a manger and an ox and an ass at Greccio on Christmas Eve of 1223. Francis believed that seeing the humble circumstances into which Jesus was born and noticing his poverty and the inconveniences of beginning life in a stable would proclaim the joy of the incarnation with a new directness. Celano writes that, "simplicity was honored, poverty was exalted, humility was commended" (I Cel 85).

Celano summed up what the significance was of that Christmas with the words, "Greccio was made, as it were, a new Bethlehem" (I Cel 85). To understand the implications of that statement, we need to step back a bit. As Jean Leclercq has convincingly and beautifully demonstrated in his *The Love of Learning and the Desire for God*, the theology that developed in the monasteries of Western Europe was experiential.[1] In the simplest terms, its purpose was for people to *experience* rather than only gain knowledge of God and the events of salvation history. The most sophisticated exposition of this monastic experiential theology is found in the writings of the Cistercian Bernard of Clairvaux (d. 1152). However, I prefer to examine a work of Aelred of Rievaulx (d.1167) because it so clearly illustrates the goals of this mode of theological inquiry. In a meditation written for his sister, a recluse, he counsels her to meditate on the nativity in the following words:

> Next with all your devotion accompany the Mother as she makes her way to Bethlehem. Take shelter in the inn with her, be present and help her as she gives birth, and when the infant is laid in the manger break out into words of exultant joy together with Isaiah and cry: "A child has been born to us, a son given to us." Embrace that sweet crib, let love overcome your reluctance, affection drive out fear. Put your lips to those most sacred feet, kiss them again and again.[2]

[1]Tr. Catharine Misrahi (New York: Fordham University Press, rpt. 1974), esp. pp. 233-286.

[2]"A Rule of Life for a Recluse" in Aelred of Rievaulx, *Treatises; the Pastoral Prayer, Cistercian Fathers Series*, #2 (Kalamazoo, MI: Cistercian Publications, 1971), p. 81.

Using the most direct language possible, William is saying that he wants his sister not merely to know things about Jesus' birth but rather in some way to experience it. She is to create in her mind the setting and try to use her imagination to place herself at the great events of salvation history.

We often think of an event as something that happened once in the past and is complete. However, Francis did not understand the birth of Jesus in that way. It is still possible to experience that event as well as to learn about it and commemorate it. Furthermore, the nativity was not an isolated event. Many events that occurred before the incarnation pointed to it, and the nativity itself points to Christ's coming both in the present and in the future. One cannot separate completely Christ's coming in Bethlehem, Christ's daily coming into our lives, and Christ's return in glory. Perhaps we moderns require more explanation of the intermediate coming of Christ than the other two. Bernard of Clairvaux wrote about it in a Christmas sermon:

> ... it is in Bethlehem of Juda Jesus is born, and study how each one of you may make himself a Bethlehem of Juda, for thus He will not disdain to be born in you also.... If, finally, thou livest by faith, ... thou art now become a Bethlehem, and comparatively fit to receive the Lord.[3]

One can receive Christ into one's heart by proper preparation. Thus, the past, present, and future are intimately related parts of a whole.

This monastic experiential theology was developed both by and for monks. The Cistercian monks were cloistered and did not often go forth into the world to preach to the laity. Of course, there were Cistercians who became bishops and even a twelfth-century Cistercian pope. Thus, monastic experiential theology was not unknown beyond cloister and chapterhouse, but it was

[3]*St. Bernard's Sermons for the Seasons and Principal Festivals of the Year* tr. a priest of Mt. Melleray (Westminster, MD: Newman Press, 1921), v. 1, p. 315. This is from Bernard's first sermon for Christmas Eve; his sixth sermon for Christmas Eve also develops this theme of Christ coming into the hearts of those who prepare to receive Him.

not adapted widely for use outside the monastery.

We will never know to what extent Francis was aware of the principles of monastic theology and how much of his own spirituality was intuited. What is clear is that Francis' spirituality was experiential and that he developed it in such a way as to make it accessible to those not trained in or for the cloistered life. One way that he helped to make the incarnation real and immediate at Greccio was to use props—the ox, ass, and manger. Francis tried with words in his sermon on Christmas Eve (the text does not survive) but also with the setting to help people not only to celebrate an event of twelve hundred years ago but to open their hearts for the coming of Christ into them. As Thomas of Celano wrote in 1228, only five years after the event: "Greccio was made, as it were, a new Bethlehem" (I Cel 85).

Although what Francis did on Christmas Eve, 1223, is at some level of consciousness derived at least in part from Cistercian theology, it is also profoundly original and influential. Ewert Cousins, a distinguished historian of spirituality and mysticism, has labelled Francis' contribution "the mysticism of the historical event."[4] Much of the mystical tradition in the West derived from Neo-platonic mysticism, in part through the writings of St. Augustine. This type of mysticism is ahistorical and world-transcending. The variety of mystical experience Francis seeks for himself and others at Greccio begins with historical and concrete dimensions of life. Francis wants us not to remember the event so much as to experience it for ourselves. One way to begin is to try to recall and even "stage" as much as possible how the original event looked to those who were participants.Through our presence at an event such as the incarnation, we come to perceive God's plan for salvation as present because God reveals himself in history. Beginning with our entering into an event such as the nativity and perceiving God's plan, we are led to union with God. As Cousins points out, the mysticism of the historical event is related to nature mysticism. Our union with nature or with a

[4]"Francis of Assisi: Christian Mysticism at the Crossroads" in *Mysticism and Religious Traditions* ed. Steven Katz (New York: Oxford University Press, 1983), pp. 163-190 and esp. pp. 166-169.

historical event, "becomes a mode of God's communication of himself to us . . . and of our union with him by perceiving his presence in the physical world."[5]

In one sense,we can say that the events of Christmas, 1223, were important to the "democratization" of mysticism. The gift of a mystical experience was often regarded as a rare one, which God usually gave to one whose whole life was preparation or schooling for an experience of union with God. Francis' Christmas crib at Greccio proclaims that it is possible for ordinary folk who work hard and raise families to enter into union with God with the help of good preaching, good staging, and of course grace.

The way to experiencing God that Francis laid out at Greccio was of the greatest influence on Franciscan spirituality and thus on the spirituality of Western Christendom for centuries. In Francis' own century, Bonaventure wrote a devotional work called *The Tree of Life*, in which he meditates on the incarnation:

> Now, then, my soul, embrace that divine manger; press your lips upon and kiss the boy's feet. Then in your mind keep the shepherd's watch, marvel at the assembling host of angels, join in the heavenly melody, singing with your voice and heart: "Glory to God in the highest and on earth peace to men of good will."[6]

In some ways, this passage sounds remarkably like the words of Aelred quoted above. Bonaventure wrote about Francis' mysticism in a work entitled *The Soul's Journey Into God.* The abstractness of this Bonaventuran text is due to the author's attempt to take the deeds and spirituality of Francis and to fit them into the existing mystical tradition. By doing that, Bonaventure tries to use a traditional language of mystical writing. However, Bonaventure is interested not only in incorporating Francis into a tradition but also showing how Francis has contributed to and in some ways transformed or advanced the tradition.[7]

[5]*Ibid.*, pp. 167-168.

[6]Tr. Ewert Cousins in *Bonaventure* (Ramsey, NJ: Paulist Press, 1978), 4.

[7]Cousins, "Francis of Assisi: Mysticism at the Crossroads," p. 175.

Toward the end of the thirteenth century, an anonymous Franciscan author wrote the *Meditations on the Life of Christ.*[8] It was often attributed to Bonaventure in the Middle Ages, but scholars now believe that it was written shortly after his death. Its popularity in the Middle Ages is attested to by the fact that more than two hundred manuscripts survive. Here, the author tries to set the scenes of New Testament stories by embellishing the biblical texts and adding a great number of "homey" details. For example,

> When they arrived in Bethlehem they could not find an inn, because they were poor and many others had come for the same purpose [i.e., to register for the tax]. Have pity on the Lady, and watch the delicate young girl, for she was only fifteen years old, as she walks ashamed among the people, fatigued by the journey and looking for a place to rest but not being able to find it because of the crowds. By all they were sent away, the holy childlike Lady and the old man Joseph her husband. When they saw an empty cave that men used when it rained, they entered to lodge themselves. And Joseph, who was a master carpenter, possibly closed it in some way. Now pay careful attention to everything, especially as I intend to recount what the Lady revealed and disclosed, as told to me by a trustworthy holy brother of our order, to whom I think it had been revealed.
>
> At midnight on Sunday, when the hour of birth came, the Virgin rose and stood erect against a column that was there. But Joseph remained seated, downcast perhaps because he could not prepare what was necessary. Then he rose and, taking some hay from the manger, placed it at the Lady's feet and turned away. Then the Son of the eternal God came out of the womb of the mother without a murmur or lesion, in a moment; as He had been in the womb so He was now outside,

[8]Tr. Isa Ragusa and Rosalie Green (Princeton: Princeton University Press, 1961). This translation also includes numerous photographs from a fourteenth-century illuminated manuscript of the text.

> on the hay at His mother's feet. Unable to contain herself, the mother stooped to pick Him up, embraced Him tenderly and, guided by the Holy Spirit, placed Him in her lap and began to wash Him with her milk, her breasts filled by heaven. When this was done, she (wrapped Him from the veil from her head and) laid Him in the manger. The ox and the ass knelt with their mouths above the manger and breathed on the Infant as though they possessed reason and knew that the child was so poorly wrapped that He needed to be warmed, in that cold season. The mother also knelt to adore Him and to render thanks to God, saying, "I thank you, most holy Father, that you gave me your Son and I adore you, eternal God, and you, Son of the living God, my Son." Joseph adored him likewise. Then he took the pack-saddle of the ass and pulled out the stuffing of straw or hair, placing it beside the manger that the Lady might rest on it. She sat down and put the saddle at her side. Thus, the Lady of the world stayed, her face turned constantly toward the manger, her eyes fixed affectionately on her sweet Son.[9]

This long quotation illustrates some of the implications of the Christmas crib at Greccio. Not only did friars use props and art in their preaching of the gospel, but they painted pictures in words by adding quite a number of details taken as much from everyday living in the thirteenth century as from scripture or tradition. This kind of spirituality could and sometimes did devolve into sentimentalism, but it is also capable of leading to conversion and even mystical experience. The passage above also contains both detailed third person narrative and direct address to the reader. It should also be noted that the passage describing the ox and ass acting as if they possessed reason is borrowed from the way birds are usually described in accounts of Francis' sermon to the birds.

The affective spirituality of the event at Greccio developed not only in the Latin literature of the later Middle Ages but also in vernacular verse. The development of the Middle English lyric

[9]*Ibid.*, pp. 31-35.

can be traced directly to Franciscan spirituality.[10] The art of preaching also developed among the friars in accord with the principles of Greccio.

The spirituality that is reflected in the Christmas crib at Greccio was important in the development of art as well as literature. Much of late medieval and Renaissance painting combines an eye for detail and a lack of concern for historical accuracy. Artists tried to create as "real" a scene as possible by dressing biblical figures in modern clothes and showing modern implements; one thinks of a painting such as Pietro Lorenzetti's birth of the Virgin in Siena.[11] The room and furnishings in which Anna gives birth are a wonderful representation of a room in the palace of a well-to-do fourteenth-century Sienese family, but they have nothing to do with the architecture and furnishings in a home in Palestine in the first century BC. Although making old stories contemporary was a principle of medieval aesthetics long before the coming of the friars, it developed rapidly and perhaps became more effective with the advent of greater realism in the art of the centuries following the establishment of the friars. One particularly powerful example of this movement is the Sacro Monte of Varallo, north of Milan. This Franciscan site consists of forty-three chapels on a mountainside, each containing lifesize statues in wood or terra cotta of events in Christ's life. One walks up the mountain, stopping to look into each chapel and seeing these scenes consisting of several statues with extraordinarily expressive faces and an illusionistic fresco for background. This is another way for the friars to carry forth the principles Francis demonstrated by bringing the ox, ass, and manger into the church in Greccio.[12]

[10]See David Jeffrey, *Franciscan Spirituality and the Early English Lyric* (Lincoln, NE: University of Nebraska Press, 1975). For a more general discussion about Franciscan influence on the development of late medieval literature, see John Fleming, *An Introduction to the Franciscan Literature of the Middle Ages* (Chicago: Franciscan Herald Press, 1977), esp. ch. 3, 4, and 6.

[11]The painting is in the Museo dell' Opera del Duomo.

[12]The best treatment of the Sacro Monte at Varallo is William Hood, "The *Sacro Monte* of Varallo: Renaissance Art and Popular Religion" in *Monasticism and the Arts* ed. Timothy Verdon (Syracuse: Syracuse University Press, 1984), pp. 291-311. I heard a

In his account of the events of Greccio, Thomas of Celano not only describes a kind of mystical ascent but also emphasizes the conversions brought about by Francis' sermon given amidst the props he set up. We are told that Christ was brought to life again in the hearts of many who had forgotten him in their lives. Thus, the Christmas crib at Greccio not only offers the possibility to a few for transcendence, but it provides many with the impetus to turn back to God so that if they do not experience union with God in this life, they have at least prepared themselves for union after their deaths.

Celano not only describes the crib with ox and ass and the sermon Francis preached at Greccio, but he also recounts a vision one man had. He saw Francis approach the manger and pick up a child there who was in a deep sleep. In this part of the Greccio narrative, Celano is stressing that Francis had a mystical experience in that he actually held the Christ child; but Celano is also suggesting that others too are able to increase their spiritual vision because of the context that Francis created.

Christmas was such an important feast for Francis because of his Christocentric spirituality. The incarnation is the supreme statement of humility in all of history, and without God becoming man, salvation for humankind remained impossible. However, Francis' life was not only a celebration of God becoming man, but a desire to live as Christ did and ultimately to die with him. His desire for martyrdom, however, was not accomplished while among the Muslims. Rather, it came in a unique way at LaVerna, just nine months after the Christmas celebration at Greccio.

paper in which Professor Hood fruitfully applied Cousins' concept of a mysticism of the historical event to his analysis of the Sacro Monte of Varallo.

7

The Stigmatization of Saint Francis

> . . . And now I make known to you a great joy and a new thing among miracles. From the beginning of the world no such sign has been heard of except in the Son of God, who is Christ.
>
> Not long before his death our brother and father appeared as one crucified, bearing in his body five wounds which are the very Stigmata of Christ. For his hands and his feet had as it were the holes of nails, pierced through on both sides, remaining as wounds and having the blackness of nails. His side also seemed to be pierced, and often bled.[1]

In October of 1226, Brother Elias wrote these words to all the friars in his letter announcing Francis' death. They comprise the earliest written description of the stigmata of Francis, perhaps the most discussed and depicted non-biblical miracle in the history of Christianity. Since Francis had tried to conceal these wounds while he was still alive, the news must have stunned all but a handful of Francis' most intimate acquaintances. Elias was aware of how shocking and perhaps unbelievable the news of the stigmata was. Yet he was bold in proclaiming this unique gift that Francis received from God.

It is worth saying at the outset that to many people in the thirteenth century, the claim that Francis had Christ's wounds

[1]From Brother Elias' letter to the friars announcing the death of Francis: it is printed in the *Omnibus*, p. 1984.

imprinted upon him was as audacious and incredible as it appears to many people in the twentieth century. Despite Elias' emphasis on the importance of the stigmata, there is no mention of this "new thing among miracles" in Gregory IX's long canonization bull of July, 1228. This omission is especially surprising since Gregory, as Cardinal Ugolino, had been cardinal protector of the Franciscan Order and an intimate friend of Francis. Later in his pontificate, he issued several bulls about the authenticity of the stigmata, and Bonaventure reports that Gregory had not always believed in the side wound but that Francis had appeared to him in a vision to show him his error (*LM*, Part II, I, 2). However, that vision occurred before the canonization, and Bonaventure reports that after it Gregory was deeply devoted to the stigmata. Although Gregory omitted any reference to the stigmata in his canonization bull, Thomas of Celano, who had been commissioned to write an official life of Francis in conjunction with his canonization, both narrates Francis' reception of Christ's wounds and also includes a meditation on the stigmata and an allegorical interpretation of the vision that Francis had at LaVerna (I Cel 94, 114).

Apparently, there were quite a few open doubters of the stigmata outside the Franciscan Order, for in 1237 Gregory IX issued three bulls authenticating all five wounds and calling on all the faithful to recognize their reality. He also said that the stigmata were part of the evidence used to canonize Francis nine years earlier. One of these bulls was addressed to a Bohemian bishop, the second to the Dominicans, and the third to all the faithful. We know that Bishop William of Olomuc in Bohemia had ordered the removal of the stigmata from visual representations of the saint in his diocese. We can suspect that some Dominicans feared the special claims for the founder of the other chief mendicant order; later in the century, one Dominican preacher claimed that Peter Martyr and not Francis was the recipient of the stigmata.[2]

[2]There is no satisfactory discussion of the controversy over the stigmata in English. However, there is an excellent article in French. See André Vauchez, "Les Stigmates de Saint François et leurs Détracteurs dans les derniers Siècles du moyen âge," *Mélanges d' Archéologie et d' Histoire* 80 (1968): 595-625.

In the 1250s, Pope Alexander IV issued several bulls authenticating the stigmata in response to paintings being altered in Genoa and Venice and opposition in Castile and Leon. In one of these he says that he personally saw the wounds on Francis' body while the saint was still alive. In 1279, Nicholas III once again reaffirmed the reality of the stigmata in a bull. The Franciscan pope Nicholas IV issued two more bulls on the stigmata toward the end of the century and also suspended a Dominican preacher for seven years who continued to deny that Francis had received Christ's wounds.

Paintings of the saint from thirteenth-century Italy are further evidence that there was a good deal of controversy about the stigmata. The earliest dated painting of the saint, a panel by Bonaventura Berlinghieri in Pescia dated 1235, contains a large central image of the saint with round black circles on his hands and feet. The earliest panels of Francis by Margaritone d'Arezzo, who must have painted many given the fact that at least seven survive, contain small black circles on the saint's hands and feet.[3] Neither Berlinghieri's nor Margaritone's paintings show the wound in Francis' side although it was represented in a French enamel reliquary and a German stained glass window about 1230.[4] These early Italian paintings, which were commissioned by friars or their patrons for Franciscan churches, proclaim the reality of the stigmata but do not show the side wound, perhaps because to show that wound, which there was some special controversy about, would have been too daring an identification between the founder of their Order and Christ.

In all likelihood, new visual images were created in Assisi to respond to the disputes over the stigmata that occurred in the pontificates of Gregory IX and Alexander IV. In 1236, Brother Elias commissioned a large crucifix for the Basilica of San Francesco in Assisi. At the feet of Christ was a small figure of St.

[3]They are found in Arezzo (2), Castiglion Fiorentino, Montepulciano, the Vatican, Siena, and San Francesco a Ripa in Rome. All but the last represent the stigmata as small black circles in the hands and feet.

[4]The two reliquaries are in the Louvre in Paris; the window is still in the Franciscan church in Erfurt, East Germany.

Francis with the stigmata in his hands and feet corresponding to the wounds of Christ on the cross. Although this particular cross was destroyed in the seventeenth century, several derived from it make clear the essential features of this new image.[5] A panel painting attributed to the so-called St. Francis Master in the Porziuncola in Assisi is probably part of the friars' campaign against the stigmata's detractors dating from the mid 1250s. It is perhaps the earliest Italian image of Francis with the side wound depicted through a tear in the saint's habit. To draw special attention to Francis' five wounds, the saint also carries a cross and a book with the inscription that says that Francis died on "this bed." While some have tried to argue that the painting is on the board on which Francis died, the reference in the inscription is certainly to the cross, which was for Francis as well as Christ a special deathbed.[6]

Even from the second half of the thirteenth century, there are images of Francis without any wounds in his hands, feet, or side. These come not from Franciscan churches but primarily from Benedictine houses.[7] This suggests that while orders such as the Benedictines recognized Francis' sancitity, they did not necessarily accept the claims of his unique likeness to Christ and therefore his unique role in salvation history that Francis' stigmatization implies.

Having established that the stigmata were a matter of some controversy and doubt, we must look at the early narrative accounts in order to understand what all the fuss was about. In examining the event of the stigmatization and some of the early interpretations of it, we will discover why some doubted the authenticity of Francis' wounds and also why this was the central event in the life of Il Poverello.

[5]There are crosses derived from the one commissioned by Elias in Santa Chiara, Assisi; Florence (private collection); Arezzo; Montefalco; Spello; Gualdo Tadino; Nocera Umbra; Bologna; and Faenza.

[6]The great Franciscan poet Jacopone da Todi, writing ca. 1300, spoke in one of his *Lauds* of the "bed of the cross." See Jacopone da Todi, *The Lauds* tr. Serge and Elizabeth Hughes (Ramsey, NJ: Paulist Press, 1982), #42.

[7]The best example is a fresco from a Benedictine chapel at Bominaco in the Abruzzi, which can be firmly dated to ca. 1263.

Portrait of St. Francis by the St. Francis Master, ca.1255. Assisi, Museum of the Porziuncola. This is probably the first Italian painting to show the side wound of Francis and was most likely commissioned at a time when some in the Church doubted the reality of the stigmata. The side wound is prominent, seen through a tear in the saint's habit. Francis carries a cross, further identifying his wounds with the experience of Christ's death on the cross. The inscription says that Francis lived and died here. Some have thought that the painting is done on the board that Francis died on. However, the "here" almost certainly refers to the cross; thus, this text also points toward Francis' stigmata and his experience of Christ's passion.

We begin with Thomas of Celano's account in his *Vita Prima*, written only about four years after the stigmatization occurred (I Cel 94). Undoubtedly, Celano spoke to Brother Leo, who was with Francis on retreat at the time of the stigmatization, as well as with men such as Elias who had seen the wounds in Francis' body while he still was alive. Francis had gone to the mountain in southern Tuscany called LaVerna, which had been "given" to him by Count Orlando of Chiusi della Verna. He was living out a forty-day "lent" in honor of St. Michael the Archangel which had begun after the feast of the Assumption. While in prayer, he had a vision of a crucified man like a seraph, wrapped in six wings. When Francis saw this, he did not understand what it meant. Celano tells us that Francis rejoiced because the seraph looked on him so lovingly but was also sad and afraid because it was nailed to a cross. In this earliest version of the vision, Francis was unsure what had happened but reacted with joy in the reception of a heavenly apparition and compassion for the seraph's suffering. The idea of compassion is important and must be understood literally. To have compassion is to share in another's passion. Since Francis shared here in the compassion of the seraph, clearly a symbol of Christ crucified, he is in some real way sharing the experience of Christ's own death.

Francis only discovered what this vision meant when he stood up after the seraph disappeared. At that time, wounds began to form in his hands and feet and side. Celano describes these in great detail. The marks in Francis' hands and feet consisted of flesh forming on the palms of his hands and tops of his feet as black heads of nails. On the opposite sides, flesh formed as the twisted ends of nails. The side was like a lance wound, and it bled for the rest of the saint's life. Thus, in the two years between the apparition of the seraph at LaVerna and the saint's death, Francis was constantly being crucified with Christ. The vision was not of a moment but introduced Francis to two years of excruciating pain and unspeakable joy—physical pain and the pain of knowing what Jesus suffered, and joy in the privilege of sharing this most intimate experience with his Lord.

Celano's narrative is rather short and matter-of-fact. However, when he describes the discovery of the stigmata by the brothers after Francis' death, he presents a meditation on and interpretation of the marks imprinted on the saint's flesh at LaVerna. Celano emphasizes, like Elias had, that this was indeed a new miracle. He describes the wounds again in great detail and refers to them as signs of martyrdom. The concept of Francis-as-martyr is an important one. In Acts of the Apostles, the stoning of Stephen is consciously paralleled with the crucifixion (Acts 7:54-60); to be a martyr is the ultimate act of obedience and conformity to Christ. This is nicely illustrated in a fifth-century mosaic in Ravenna of the martyrdom of St. Lawrence. He approaches the fiery gridiron on which he was to be martyred, carrying his cross; for Lawrence, that gridiron *is* his cross, his device of torture which, like Christ's, becomes his sign of triumph over death. Francis too is a martyr, but he had the special privilege of receiving his martyrdom in the same way Christ had. And he had the privilege not of a moment of suffering in order to triumph over death, but of two years of feeling the nails in his hands and feet and bleeding from the side. Francis had become a "living cross" (I Cel 114).

Celano brings his thoughts about the stigmatization together in a wonderful allegory of the meaning of the six wings. The two above the seraph's head represent pure intention and upright actions. These must always go together, for good works without right intentions are not pleasing to God. The second pair of wings concerns charity for one's neighbor; one represents bringing him/her God's word and the other providing earthly help. The final pair of wings—contrition and confession—are needed because of man's inability to avoid sin. This allegorical reading of the wings of the seraph brilliantly brings several key elements of Francis' life together. The first pair suggests the symbiosis of active and contemplative elements. In prayer, one experiences God's love and sees his plan; only then can one really do deeds that further the coming of the kingdom of God. The second pair are the wings of ministry—presenting God's word and providing for basic needs. For Francis, these can never be divorced, for he is an apostolic man and not a social worker. The third pair of wings not only represents much of the substance of Francis' preaching, the call to repentance, but also reminds us that without the humility that is required for admitting failure and asking for help, there can be no authentic living out of the gospel. Although Celano presents his allegory of the three pairs of wings in the order I have just discussed them, they should also be looked at in reverse order. None of the higher callings of the Christian will occur until one recognizes his/her sinfulness and the inability to do anything about it on one's own. Once a person has experienced grace, God's undeserved gift, he/she can then and only then share it with his/her brothers and sisters both in preaching the word and in works of mercy. The apostolic follower of Christ must, however, renew him/herself by listening to God, experiencing Him directly, and then returning refreshed to do good deeds with the right intentions. Without this, means easily become ends and apparent good deeds become self-serving acts.

Another early version of the stigmatization is contained in the panel painting of Bonaventura Berlinghieri in Pescia dated 1235. As far as we know, this was the first visual representation of the vision at LaVerna. The artist has telescoped time in order to show both the appearance of the seraph and Francis marked with the wounds of Christ in his hands and feet. The most important element of this painting is the position of the figure of Francis. He kneels with his hands together in a gesture of prayer. The resonances of this iconography help us to understand the message the artist wished to convey. The figure kneeling on the mountain is probably derived from the iconography of Christ in the garden of Gethsemani. Thus, Francis humbly responds to the cup that he must drink from in the same way as Christ did. Francis' reception of the stigmata is the sign of his acceptance of God's will, whatever that entails, just as Christ's crucifixion was carried out after he said to the Father: "Thy will be done."

All of the artists who depicted the stigmatization based on I Celano created ways of linking the seraph and Francis. Berlinghieri made a thick gold band that connected the two figures; however, this was not particularly successful because it was difficult to see against a gold background. Other painters, such as the artist of a panel painting in the church of Santa Croce in Florence and also of a separate stigmatization now in the Uffizi, used three narrow gold bands connecting the seraph and the nimbus of Francis. There are obvious trinitarian connotations

The stigmatization from the panel of Bonaventura Berlinghieri. This is the earliest representation of the stigmatization. The seraph is shown coming from heaven, represented by concentric circles. Francis kneels in prayer on the mountain. He already bears the wounds in his hands and feet although Celano says that they only appeared after the seraph disappeared. A gold band connects the seraph and Francis. The architecture is an iconographic convention rather than a depiction of buildings at La Verna. The placement of Francis borrows from the iconography of Christ in the garden of Gethsemani. Thus, the artist has cleverly linked Christ's and Francis' passions.

here, reminding us that this is a vision sent from God.

In panel paintings containing the stigmatization in Pistoia and Orte, both dating from the 1250s, Francis kneels in front of a cave. The verbal source for this detail is the liturgical sequence "Sanctitatis nova signa" (New sign of sanctity) attributed to Thomas of Celano. It is worth turning to this text to gain another perspective on the meaning of Francis' reception of Christ's wounds.[8] In the first three verses, the word "new" appears five times. Celano speaks of a new flock with a new law; thus, the stigmatization is not only a miracle testifying to Francis' great sanctity, but it also is in some way meaningful for the Order of St. Francis. Bonaventure later develops this idea. While the stigmatization is a new sign of sanctity, it is at the same time a renewal of the decrees of God and a return to the Gospel. Thus, that which is new takes its meaning from what happened at Calvary and suggests a *re*forming of the Church. The stigmatization validates the life of the friars, which is nothing but the return to the life of the apostles. In describing the event at LaVerna, Celano emphasizes Francis' solitude and describes him hidden in a grotto. When describing the seraph, he refers to it as, "the great king." While Celano did not identify the crucified seraph with Christ in the *Vita Prima*, he does so specifically in "Sanctitatis nova signa." Celano tells us that Francis and the seraph spoke and that the seraph revealed many secrets. Then, Celano tells us that, "Francis contemplates the future in sublime ecstasy." Thus, Celano brings all time—past, present, and future—together at LaVerna. What happened at LaVerna was something new that derived its meaning from something old, and it gave Francis a prophetic vision of the future. Although there may be apocalyptic allusions here, I think that primarily this vision of the future refers first to Francis' salvation and second to the role of the Order in rebuilding the Church. There is also an obvious parallel with the events at Greccio on Christmas Eve, 1223, where past, present, and future come together.

[8]Unfortunately, I do not know of an English translation of the "Sanctitatis Nova Signa."

That Francis received this prophetic vision on a mountain in a cave links the saint to the prophet Elijah. In I Kings 19, Elijah spent forty days (like Francis' "lent" at LaVerna) on Mt. Horeb, where Moses had received the law after staying with God there for forty days.[9] Celano emphasizes the new law of the friars, which is the renewal of the gospel, in "Sanctitatis nova signa." Elijah was in a cave when God spoke to him; he stood at the entrance of the cave, and God asked him why he was there. Elijah replied that he was there because of his zeal for the Lord, and that in the present, there were many who had forsaken God's law. The Lord sent him back into the world and commanded him to anoint Elisha as his successor. Celano's use of the cave to link Francis to Elijah is brilliant and tells us a great deal about how we are to understand the stigmatization. First, it associates Francis with the Old Testament prophetic tradition but also to the New Testament prophet John the Baptist, who is the "destined Elijah" (Mt 11:14), and who came, "possessed by the spirit and power of Elijah" (Lk 1:17). The forty days of both Moses and Elijah on Mt. Horeb, where God gave the law of the Old Testament, are linked to the forty-day fast of Christ before he gave the new law in the Sermon on the Mount (Mt 4:2). Both of these events are linked to the stigmatization by the forty days and the proclamation of a new law, as Celano emphasizes in "Sanctitatis nova signa." Just as Elijah experienced the presence of God, so did Francis. Elijah's experience was linked to the past by its location on Mt. Horeb, but it was also concerned with the future. So was Francis' experience linked to Mt. Horeb and to Calvary but also to the future, where Francis' charism was to be passed on to others doing battle with the powerful enemies of God. As Elijah was commanded to anoint Elisha, so was Francis by his rule and example to commission a whole army of friars prepared for the dangers of doing battle because people had forsaken God's covenant.

As with other aspects of Francis' life, the various strands present in the works of Thomas of Celano are brilliantly synthe-

[9]There are various versions of Moses' reception of the law on Mt. Horeb (or Sinai); the forty-day stay followed by the reception of the tablets is recorded in Exodus 34:27-28.

sized and explored further by Bonaventure. In the *Legenda Maior*, one is always aware of the stigmatization as the key to understanding who Francis is and what his Order is all about. In the prologue and in virtually every chapter, we are called to reflect on the stigmata in a number of different contexts. After Bonaventure narrates the events at LaVerna in chapter thirteen, he summarizes all the visions of Francis and Christ Crucified that led up to the appearance of the seraph on LaVerna, making clear that the stigmatization is the culmination of Francis' spiritual pilgrimage to God (*LM* XIII, 10).

As discussed previously, the chapter describing the stigmatization and the one that precedes it begin with a discussion of the relationship of the active and contemplative dimensions of Francis' life. While chapter 12 goes on to discuss Francis' ministry of preaching, chapter 13 describes Francis' retreat to LaVerna and the vision that he received there. One context in which we should therefore consider the stigmatization is as a definitive statement about action and contemplation. The stigmatization is both the fruit of contemplation and the authentication of ministry.

As a framework to the actual narration of the events at LaVerna, Bonaventure borrows phrases from the synoptic gospels' accounts of the Transfiguration of Christ.[10] In fact, twice in the narrative, Bonaventure writes of Francis' transformation into the true image of Christ (*LM* XIII, 3, 5).

The narrative of the vision follows rather closely the account in I Celano. However, Bonaventure does add after his description of the apparition that it was Christ under the appearance of a seraph (*sub specie seraph* in the original Latin). This detail is significant. In I Celano, Francis saw the vision of a man; in the *Legenda Maior*, his vision is of Christ; and Francis understands by grace how to "read" this vision to know that he is experiencing Christ Crucified. Since the term *specie* is used in thirteenth-century theology in the context of the eucharist (Christ is present under the species of bread and wine), we can appreciate Francis' faith in

[10]For example, he borrows from Mt 17:1 in *LM* XIII, 1. Bonaventure also borrows from Exod 31:18, which describes Moses' descent from the mountain, in *LM* XIII, 5.

penetrating beneath the appearance of the seraph to the reality of Christ, just as one must do in recognizing with the eyes of faith that Christ is really present in a piece of bread.

In the earliest paintings of the stigmatization, the artists used the conventional representation of a seraph as the basis for depicting what appeared to Francis. In the fresco of the stigmatization in the Upper Church in Assisi, ascribed by tradition to Giotto, the figure wrapped in the wings of the seraph is Christ, recognizable both by his general appearance and his cruciform nimbus. Thus, as the verbal tradition developed in the thirteenth century, so did the visual representation of Francis' vision at LaVerna.

Bonaventure understands the stigmatization as a unique martyrdom. In his chapter about Francis' quest for martyrdom in the Middle East, he concluded with a quotation from the liturgy for the feast of St. Martin of Tours, one of the Church's earliest saints who was not martyred: "The persecutor's sword did not take [him] away, and yet [he] did not lose the palm of martyrdom" (*LM* IX, 9). Thus, Francis' reception of Christ's wounds is a special kind of living martyrdom, for he received the same wounds that Christ died from in only three hours, yet he lived for two years with them.

When Bonaventure describes Francis' descent from LaVerna, he describes him as bearing the image of the crucified, not on tablets of stone or a panel of wood, but in his body (*LM* XIII, 5). It is God the artist who created this image of Christ, not a human writer or craftsman. Francis is a unique icon or image of God because he is living rather than made of inanimate material. However, Bonaventure knows that his readers cannot experience that image in the same way as Brother Illuminato and the future Pope Alexander IV, who had seen the wounds in the living body of Francis, or as Clare and others, who had seen them before Francis' body was placed in his tomb. How then will friars and the people in general know of this living image of Christ? The answer is that Francis will be known through words (tablets of stone) and pictures (panels of wood). Thus we know about the living image of Christ that is Francis by images made of inanimate things (marks of ink on a page and colors on a piece of wood); this parallels that marvellous statement discussed in chapter five that we must *read* that Christ prayed more than he read.

The wounds of Christ imprinted on Francis' body also confirm that Francis is indeed a knight of Christ (*LM* XIII, 9). A knight in the service of his lord carries the lord's coat of arms. Francis' Lord is Christ, so as his knight he carries his coat of arms—the wounds he received on the cross. When Francis stripped himself before the bishop, he traced a cross on the poor garment that he received that day to cover his nakedness. Little could he have realized that this was a foreshadowing of putting on Christ (cf. Eph 4:24) in even a more literal and profound way.

In addition to Francis being Christ's vassal, he is also Christ's herald. Bonaventure tells us that just after Francis' renunciation of worldly things before the bishop, he was accosted by robbers who asked him who he was. Francis replied: "I am the herald of the great King" (*LM* II, 5). Those words he spoke were prophetic, for the wounds of Christ mark Francis as Christ's herald. A herald goes before a king on a journey, announcing his arrival, and he is recognized because he carries the king's banner. Francis is preparing the way for the Lord, "a way of light and peace into the hearts of [Christ's] faithful" (*LM* Prologue, I). Francis himself is the banner of Christ, for he carries the distinguishing sign of his Lord.

The wounds of Christ are also Christ's seal—that is, His signature. I will consider the prophetic and mystical dimensions of the seal later. For now, I want to focus on the more literal sense of the stigmata as seals. In the Middle Ages, a seal was a sign of authenticity. If one signed a document in an official capacity, he/she also attached a wax seal. The piece of metal or wood that made the impression on the hot wax was intricately designed so as to be almost impossible to duplicate. Thus, if a charter carried the seal of a particular baron, one could have confidence that it was not a forgery. In 1223, Pope Honorius III issued a bull confirming the Rule for the Franciscan Order; that document, complete with papal seal, is still preserved in the Basilica of San Francesco in Assisi. For Bonaventure, this papal bull was important in its own right but was also another prefiguration of the stigmatization:

> To confirm [the Rule] with greater certainty by God's own testimony . . . the stigmata of our Lord Jesus were imprinted upon him by the finger of the living God, as the bull or seal of Christ, the Supreme Pontiff, for the complete confirmation of this rule and the approval of its author (*LM* IV, 11).

Just as Christ's vicar attested to the authenticity of the Rule by affixing his seal to a written bull, so Christ himself attested to the authenticity of Francis' way of life by marking him with his seal of authenticity. Thus, one important dimension of the stigmatization is that it presents objective evidence that Francis' life is uniquely Christlike and therefore worthy of veneration and imitation. The stigmatization is God's making public what He had given Francis many years before when he impressed Christ Crucified in his heart (*LM* I, 5). And with this sealing of Francis, as Bonaventure points out, "[his] words and deeds will rightly be accepted by all as authentic and beyond reproach" (*LM* XIII, 9). The stigmatization is for us as much as it is for Francis.

Although Bonaventure lays out a structure for the *Legenda Maior* in his Prologue based on the number three, he reveals to us at the end of the chapter concerning the stigmata that there is also a sevenfold structure to the relationship of Francis to Christ Crucified (*LM* XIII, 10). This has a specifically mystical significance that will be discussed below. It parallels the six days of creation followed by a day of rest and also reminds us of the seven times Christ spoke from the cross.[11] Bonaventure's purpose in recalling the six encounters of Francis and Christ Crucified before the stigmatization thus reveals a mystical structure to Francis' life, a pattern that is almost impossible to discern without the stigmatization to guide us back into Francis' life.

In the first of these visions of Francis and Christ Crucified, the young Francis sees a palace full of weapons which display Christ's coat of arms, the cross (*LM* I, 3). Francis misinterprets the vision to mean that he will become a great warrior. In the second vision,

[11] If one examines all the gospel accounts of the crucifixion, there is a total of seven different words or statements that Christ uttered.

Francis saw not just the cross but Christ crucified on a cross (*LM* I, 5). Bonaventure tells us that from this time on, the memory of the passion was always in his heart. The third vision is the famous one of the painted crucifix at San Damiano telling Francis to go and rebuild his church (*LM* II, 1). In this vision, which he also took quite literally at first, Francis both sees and hears Christ crucified. In other words, the vision becomes more intimate as we move forward in time. These three all take place before Francis' dramatic conversion when he stripped himself naked before the bishop of Assisi.

After Francis became "a crucified man," as Bonaventure refers to him in the passage describing his renunciation before the bishop (*LM* II, 4), the type of vision of Francis and Christ Crucified changes radically. Instead of Christ appearing to Francis, the visions are of Francis appearing with the cross to others. Brother Silvester saw a golden cross coming from Francis' mouth that drove a dragon away from Assisi (*LM* III, 5). Francis had at the time of his conversion put on Christ, and Silvester's vision is a manifestation of Christ Crucified dwelling in Francis. Later, Brother Pacificus saw Francis with two shining swords in the form of a cross extending from head to toe and arm to arm (*LM* IV, 9). Finally, Brother Monaldus saw Francis appear to a chapter meeting at Arles during a sermon by Anthony of Padua about the inscription on the cross: "Jesus of Nazareth, King of the Jews." Francis appeared lifted up in midair, his arms extended as though on a cross. . . ." (*LM* IV, 10). In these three visions, we can see how Francis more and more resembles Christ Crucified. In fact, one can think in this context of Thomas of Celano's statement that Francis, "was always on the cross" (I Cel 115).

For Bonaventure, Francis' whole life was a preparation for the mystical union with Christ that took place at LaVerna, and the signs of that union are in part for us to be able to know of the genuineness of Francis' whole life and his unique experience of Christ.

When Bonaventure went to LaVerna after his election as Minister General (before he wrote the *Legenda Maior*), he reflected on the stigmata and wrote *The Soul's Journey Into God*, one of the classics of Christian mystical literature. He says that,

> . . . while reflecting on [the vision of a winged Seraph in the form of the Crucified], I saw at once that this vision represented our father's [Francis'] rapture in contemplation and the road by which this rapture is reached.
>
> The six wings of the seraph can rightly be taken to symbolize the six levels of illumination by which, as if by steps or stages, the soul can pass over to peace through ecstatic elevations of Christian wisdom. There is no other path but through the burning love of the Crucified, a love which so transformed Paul into Christ when he "was carried up to the third heaven" [II Cor 12:2] that he could say, "With Christ I am nailed to the cross. I live, now not I, but Christ lives in me" [Gal 2:19-20]. This love also so absorbed the soul of Francis that his spirit shone through his flesh when for two years before his death he carried in his body the sacred stigmata of the passion. The six wings of the seraph, therefore, symbolize the six steps of illumination that begin from creatures and lead up to God, whom no one rightly enters except through the Crucified (Prologue, 3).

The most beautiful visual expression of the mystical dimension of the stigmatization is Giotto's wonderful painting of the event above the entrance to the Bardi Chapel in the Franciscan church of Santa Croce in Florence. In it, we clearly see the six wings of the seraph and Christ Crucified within them. Giotto has positioned the wings in such a manner that they block out part of Christ's body from our view; however, the entire body of Christ is visible to Francis. In order to experience Christ as Francis did at LaVerna, we too must go about an orderly progression of illumination. This fresco is one of seven in Giotto's Bardi Chapel cycle and is above the entrance to the chapel, while the other six stories decorate the walls of the chapel itself. Although only one of the six visions of Francis and Christ Crucified—the appearance at the chapter at Arles—is depicted in this cycle, Giotto has kept the number symbolism of six steps leading to Francis' union with Christ at LaVerna.

In the upper left corner of Giotto's stigmatization is a falcon. This detail comes directly from the *Legenda Maior* and sheds light on another dimension of the event (*LM* VIII, 10). In the chapter entitled "On His Affectionate Piety and How Irrational Creatures Were Affectionate Toward Him," Bonaventure tells about a falcon that built a nest near where Francis was living when he was at LaVerna, and it woke him or let him sleep according to what Francis needed. For Bonaventure, this relationship between the falcon and the saint was not accidental but providential:

> There certainly seems to have been a divine prophecy . . . in the song of the falcon—a prophecy of the time when this praiser and worshiper of God would be lifted up on the wings of contemplation and there would be exalted with a Seraphic vision (*LM* VIII,10).

From this passage, we can understand the stigmatization as a most profound truth prophesied in nature. A good reader of nature will see in this act of the falcon a prefiguration or prophecy of what took place at LaVerna later. In this way too is the stigmatization the culmination and authentication of Francis' entire life, since Francis himself was the best reader of nature and a teacher to others who would read it.

However, Francis' reception of the stigmata is not only prophesied in nature, for Bonaventure emphasizes in the *Prologue* to the *Legenda Maior* that Francis is prophesied in the Book of Revelation under the image of the angel bearing the seal of the living God (Rev 7:2). Thus, God has revealed the profound mystery of the stigmata both in nature and scripture.

This identification of Francis with the angel bearing the seal of the living God forms the basis for an apocalyptic perspective on Francis because this angel's appearance in Revelation is immediate preparation for the breaking of the seventh and final seal. It is not within the scope of this work to trace Bonaventure's apocalypticism;[12] however, let me briefly suggest that Bonaventure puts

[12]Professors Ronald Herzman and Richard Emmerson are currently completing a study of apocalyptic thought in the writings of Bonaventure.

Francis' life into a metahistorical perspective. Francis is not simply another reformer or founder of an Order, although he is of course both of those things; his life is a significant event in salvation history. Just as John the Baptist came to prepare the way for God incarnate, so does Francis come to prepare for Christ's final return in glory. Bonaventure's evidence for this unique role for Francis is the five wounds of Christ imprinted in the saint's body.

From the creation of the Christmas crib at Greccio, we were able to discern what Ewert Cousins calls the mysticism of the historical event.[13] At LaVerna, this type of mystical experience is both confirmed and also put into the context of more traditional forms of Christian mysticism. Francis is mystically present at the crucifixion of his Lord; the reception of Christ's wounds makes this abundantly clear. Beginning only a decade after Francis' death, it became common to depict him at the foot of Christ's cross.[14] Although Francis is tiny compared to Christ in order to make clear which event is central to all salvation history, the special relationship between Christ and Francis is obvious since they both bear the same wounds. Thus, Francis' experience of the crucified Christ at LaVerna is the supreme expression of this new form of mysticism. The experience of being in the presence of Christ crucified became the goal of Franciscan spirituality. The epigraph of Bonaventure's *The Tree of Life* is Galatians 2:19: "With Christ I am nailed to the cross." Later in the same work, Bonaventure writes:

> And then transfixed with nails, he appeared to you as your beloved cut through with wound upon wound in order to heal you. "Who will grant me that my request should come about

[13]See Cousins' "Francis of Assisi: Christian Mysticism at the Crossroads" in *Mysticism and Religous Traditions* ed. Steven Katz (New York: Oxford University Press, 1983), pp. 163-190.

[14]The cross of 1236, originally in San Francesco in Assisi, has been destroyed. Those derived from it are listed in note 5 of this chapter. The parallel between Francis' and Christ's wounds is particularly clear in the cross hanging over the high altar of San Francesco in Arezzo.

> and that God will give me what I long for" [Job 6:8], that having been totally transpierced in both mind and flesh, I may be fixed with my beloved to the yoke of the cross (*The Tree of Life* 26).

While the LaVerna experience is in some ways quite different from the mysticism that negates anything physical, Bonaventure succeeds in incorporating it into more traditonal, Neo-platonic inspired mysticism. In his *The Soul's Journey Into God*, Bonaventure's last chapter discusses the end of the mystical journey that he described in the six previous chapters:

> After our mind had beheld God outside itself and through his vestiges and in his vestiges, within itself through its image and in his image, and above itself through the similitude of the divine Light shining above us and in the Light itself, insofar as this is possible in our state as wayfarers and through the exercise of our mind, when finally in the sixth stage our mind reaches that point where it contemplates in the First and Supreme Principle and in the mediator of God and men, Jesus Christ, those things whose likenesses can in no way be found in creatures and which surpass all penetration by the human intellect, it now remains for our mind, by contemplating these things, to transcend and pass over not only this sense world but even itself (*The Soul's Journey Into God* VII, 1).

Only a few lines later, Bonaventure relates this transcendent experience to the stigmatization:

> This was shown also to blessed Francis, when in ecstatic contemplation on the height of the mountain—where I have thought out these things I have written—there appeared to him a six-winged Seraph fastened to a cross, as I and several others heard in that very place from his companion who was with him then [Leo]. There he passed over into God in ecstatic contemplation and became an example of perfect contemplation as he had previously been of action, like another Jacob and Israel, so that through him, more by example than by

> word, God might invite all truly spiritual men to this kind of passing over and spiritual ecstasy.
>
> In this passing over, if it is to be perfect, all intellectual activities must be left behind and the height of our affection must be totally transferred and transformed into God. This, however, is mystical and most secret, which no one knows except him who receives it, no one receives except him who desires it, and no one desires except him who is inflamed in his very marrow by the fire of the Holy Spirit whom Christ sent into the world (*The Soul's Journey Into God* VII, 3-4).

In *The Soul's Journey Into God*, Bonaventure has both situated Francis' experience into the traditional understanding of mysticism and enlarged the tradition to include Francis' contribution of a mysticism rooted in the experience of the incarnate Word, or what has been called the mysticism of the historical event. Ewert Cousins thinks of Bonaventure's contribution to mystical thought in the highest terms: "What Thomas [Aquinas] achieved for Aristotle in theology, Bonaventure did for Francis in mysticism."[15]

Elias knew from the time that he learned of the stigmata that they were more than ordinary marks of sanctity. However, he and Celano saw neither all the implications nor all the ways that the event at LaVerna brought together the major elements of Francis' spirituality. It was only in the experiences of the Order and in the minds of geniuses such as Bonaventure and Giotto that all the significance of Francis' vision on LaVerna became clear to the people of God.

[15]p. 168.

Conclusion

In this study, I have to a great extent ignored the development of the Franciscan Order and Francis' relationship with the hierarchy of the Roman Church. However, these topics deserve some consideration even in a study that primarily focuses on the saint's spirituality.

Francis was not a terribly gifted administrator. The vocations of prophet and manager are rarely found together. He did not deal well with abstractions, and government at any level involves a lot of abstractions. Francis was used to dealing with this or that brother rather than with the brotherhood. He also was not a particularly good legislator. Establishing procedures and regulations was foreign to Francis' spontaneity. He did not think of establishing a novitiate until he had no real choice. For Francis, it was enough for someone to want to live the gospel life and to leave his possessions behind. In precisely that way did John the Simple become a friar (II Cel 190). Even regarding the question of poverty, Francis did not think of it as essentially a legal matter or have a definition that would have made much sense to a canon lawyer. Francis insisted on absolute poverty, but he in some way accepted the gift of the mountain of LaVerna from Count Orlando of Chiusi della Verna.[1] The need for the division of the friars into provinces and the establishment of regular meetings

[1]The source is from the fourteenth century, but it probably is based on a genuine tradition. See the second part of the *Fioretti* entitled "The Considerations of the Holy Stigmata," First Consideration. For the genuineness of the tradition, see John Moorman, *A History of the Franciscan Order from its Origins to the Year 1517* (Oxford: Clarendon Press, 1968), p. 26.

(general chapters) must also have perplexed Francis. What the friars were called to do was for Francis quite simple—live the life prescribed in the gospel for the apostles and in imitation of Christ. What that meant was clear to Francis. Why did there have to be long meetings to discuss it?

Despite his reservations and doubts about the organization of the Order, Francis did agree to have a novitiate, hold general chapters, and write a Rule in language that made sense to canon lawyers.[2] He did not reject decisions concerning the Friars Minor made by the pope or the Order's cardinal protector, although his own way would have been different. The tension caused him pain, but he never wavered in his belief in the authority of the ecclesiastical hierarchy. At least to this extent, Francis has to be praised as the founder of an Order.

Francis' vision of the call to live the gospel life did not end with his concern for the Friars Minor. It was Francis who tonsured Clare, the great saint and founder of female Franciscanism. She too struggled with the authorities who wanted to cloister her and endow her convent. After the Clares were established at San Damiano, which Francis had helped to rebuild, they received less guidance and fewer visits from Francis and his closest circle of brothers than they would have liked. Francis was himself quite ambivalent about what his attitude should be toward these holy women. Even without his day-to-day guidance, it was still he that inspired the movement and provided the model for poverty.[3]

Francis also founded an order for those living in the world who could not abandon everything to enter the Friars Minor or the Clares. The so-called Third Order provided an opportunity for members of the laity with families and jobs to experience the Franciscan calling and charism. In many towns, members of the

[2]The Rule of 1223, approved by Pope Honorius III, is printed in *Francis and Clare: The Complete Works* tr. Regis Armstrong and Ignatius Brady (Ramsey, NJ: Paulist Press, 1982), pp. 136-145.

[3]For a history of the Clares in the thirteenth century, see Moorman, pp. 32-39. Clare's writings are available in a good English translation in *Francis and Clare: The Complete Works*. A life of Clare attributed to Thomas of Celano exists in an English translation. See *The Life of St. Clare* tr. Ignatius Brady and Sister M. Frances (St.Bonaventure, NY: The Franciscan Institute, 1953).

Third Order met for prayer, communal penance, and charitable works. They provided a "support system" in a time when urban growth was creating an ever more impersonal world. Although the Third Order has gone through many changes in the intervening centuries, it has recently become revitalized as an important vehicle of the Franciscan charism in the modern world.[4]

Francis' charism thus took even in his lifetime a variety of institutional forms. No one was excluded from experiencing Francis' spirituality and strong sense of community. Today, there are numerous male and female orders that make up the family of Franciscan orders, and they are not always as familial with one another as they should be. Nevertheless, the Franciscan orders play important roles in virtually every ministry of the Church and in every place on the globe. They teach at all levels. They conduct retreats. Some live in contemplation. They serve as missionaries virtually everywhere. Friars have parishes and run hospitals. One can find friars running soup kitchens in Philadelphia, self-help programs on Indian reservations, Newman Centers at universities. Despite adaptations to the lifestyle of the twentieth century and occasional deviation from Franciscan principles, the various Franciscan institutions are forces for good in the world. One can thus conclude that despite Francis' lack of administrative ability, he is indeed the person primarily responsible for one of the great institutions of the Church.

Francis' relationship with the Roman Church is one of the most interesting facets of his life. He began his religious life literally in the arms of his bishop; he sought the approval of the pope for his little band of apostolic men. Despite these powerful images of Francis and the ecclesiastical hierarchy, it is hard to imagine more different men than Francis on one hand and Bishop Guido and Pope Innocent III on the other. Guido was a prelate constantly engaged in political machinations; he lived, like virtually all bishops, in a palace and was not particularly known for his sanctity. Innocent was probably the most powerful man in

[4]See Moorman, pp. 216-225, for the early history of the Third Order. Two "Letters to the Faithful," which concern the Third Order, are printed in *Francis and Clare: The Complete Works*, pp. 62-73.

Europe during most of his pontificate. He was a master of international diplomacy, dealing effectively with the likes of King Philip Augustus of France, King John of England, and the Holy Roman Emperor Otto IV. He lived in the splendor of the Lateran Palace. Why did Francis have so much respect for these successors of the apostles who were living so differently from the life prescribed by Christ and described in Acts of the Apostles? To some extent, the question contains the answer: these men were the successors of the apostles, and thus received their authority from God. Francis was humble enough to recognize his own sins and failings and was unwilling to judge others. Christ said in his Sermon on the Mount that one should not look at the speck of sawdust in another's eye because he/she has a great plank in his/her own (Mt 7:3). Francis would not see himself free to disregard this gospel precept any more than he was free to ignore the call to poverty. Francis recognized that those in different callings in the Church were the recipients of different graces. For example, he always admonished his friars to treat even bad priests with the greatest respect, for they had the gift of receiving and administering the body and blood of Christ.[5] Isaiah prophesied a time when animals such as lions and lambs would lie down together (Isa 11:6-9); there has hardly been a moment in the history of the Church when lions and lambs have been closer than during the lives of Francis of Assisi and Innocent III.

What about the other side of the coin? Why did Bishop Guido and Innocent III so warmly embrace Francis? We must not underestimate the uneasiness the pope must have felt when he approved the friars' rule in 1209. It was inevitable that someone would have perceived the friars' apostolic way of life as a damning gloss on the lives of the successors of the apostles, the ecclesiastical hierarchy. Cardinal Ugolino must have sometimes been frustrated by Francis' unwillingness to see the organizational problems of the Order and his inability to devise enforceable and suitable solutions. It would be naive to pretend that there was no political motive in the hierarchy's support of Francis. Here was a man who

[5]See Francis' "Testament" in *Francis and Clare: The Complete Works*, p. 154.

was a living refutation of some of the claims of the Waldensians and Albigensians. He not only saved many from falling into heresy, but he also no doubt was able to win some heretics back to the Roman Church. Innocent III's historical reputation is primarily in the realm of his mastery of European politics. However, he was a serious church reformer; we should not be so cynical as to assume that he was a reformer only to advance his political goals.

None of the above answers is sufficient to explain the way the hierarchy treated Francis. We are forced to return, as always, to the person of Francis. It was simply impossible for a Christian (or perhaps anyone, given his reception by the sultan) not to be drawn to him by his genuineness, lack of pretense, and humility. It must have always been clear that he had no hidden agenda. When Francis said that all he desired was to imitate Christ, his potential adversaries were completely disarmed because there was no doubt that what he said was exactly what he wanted to do. Most people then and now almost instinctively ask questions such as, "What did he/she *really* mean?" or "what does he/she stand to gain from this?" The sources suggest to me that it was almost impossible even for a cynic or a political manipulator to ask these questions about Francis of Assisi. His genuineness and simplicity were irresistible. To say no to Francis must have seemed like saying no directly to Christ. Francis broke down the defense mechanisms of those he met. Maybe that is what Isaiah was imagining when he spoke of the lamb and the lion lying down together.

The history of Christianity can be looked at in terms of the tension between prophecy and order. Sometimes the tension has been constructive and at other times destructive. Officeholders tend to fear those who claim authority outside the structures of the institution. Prophets sometimes look upon structures as compromises at best and perhaps even enemies of the truth as they claim to understand it from God. In the first years of the thirteenth century, the prophet in his rags and the pontiff crowned with his tiara followed their callings with vigor while recognizing that there were other ways of living the Christian life. Innocent was not a threat to Francis, for the latter invariably recognized the pope's authority, sought his counsel, and obeyed his teaching. Francis did not threaten Innocent, for the pope saw the reformation of the Church linked to his support of the man in rags that he saw in a dream holding up the tottering cathedral of Rome (II Cel 17).

Francis' success as the founder of a family of orders, his adherence to the Roman Church and pontiff, and his role in the rebuilding of an imperfect institution do not explain the extraordinary appeal of this man in his own and subsequent ages. In order to do that, we must return to reflect on some of the stories that we have already examined in some detail. It is primarily in them that we can discover why Francis is so important to our own age.

When Francis learned of his call from God to rebuild the Church, he recognized two things that we too often forget. The first is that he could not treat his call to reform the Church as separate from the other facets of his and everyone's call to live the Christian life. One cannot rebuild the Church while ignoring one's weaknesses and constant need for repentance and personal reform. So often, people take great gifts and treat them as privileges that exempt them from more universal duties and obligations. The great task that God called Francis to was not an exemption from prayer, fasting, and ministry to the poor. Rather, his call to rebuild the Church was rooted in living out the calling of all Christians in a deeper and more singleminded way. Second, when Francis heard the call to rebuild the Church, he did not fully grasp what it was God required of him. He responded immediately by fixing up three collapsing church buildings on the outskirts of Assisi. Sometimes when a person perceives that God is calling him/her to some task, the response is to wait until all the pieces of the puzzle are in place. One can easily fall into the trap of saying that when God wants me to get going, He will fill me in on the details and show me exactly how to go about fulfilling his call. I do not wish to deny that prudence is a virtue, but often sloth and lack of trust masquerade under its guise. Francis perhaps had some sense that he would not be patching church walls all his life. However, it was in terms of church repair that he understood God's call at San Damiano, so he responded "yes" to God as best he could, because he trusted that God had told him as much as he could understand at that moment. Francis did not put his trust in his own cleverness but in God and responded as best he could. That is an important lesson in our sometimes overcalculating age.

As Francis stood naked before Bishop Guido, he discovered freedom. For the first time, he saw things as they are rather than as they appear to be. For most Christians, conversion does not happen in such a dramatic way. Many Christians doubt their own conversions because they have not turned to God in a sensational way; similarly, many doubt that they can experience union with God in this life because they have never had a vision. Francis' nakedness does remind us that conversion involves a radical re-orientation; it is not a matter of altering one's lifestyle or philosophy of life a bit. However, Francis' dramatic gesture neither began nor ended that day. His complete turning toward and surrender to God was a process that began when he first failed to find pleasure in the beauty of Umbria, when he left the military expedition to Apulia, when he began to go up to remote places on Monte Subasio to pray. And it did not end until he died naked on the ground outside the Porziuncola on October 3, 1226.

Francis was continually discovering the implications of a surrender to God after he renounced his earthly possessions and family. The problem many Christians have is not in making a commitment to do God's will, but in keeping it once they discover what it is they agreed to do. When Francis discovered the implications of calling all things brother or sister, he rejoiced in his discovery rather than shrank away from seeing creation as a family. When he discovered the virtue of poverty, he did not try to figure out ways of having things while still being poor; he embraced poverty's most radical implications. Many have had a flash of insight or moment of grace when they perceived God's truth, but most are not able to live out their lives without compromising what they know. It is Francis' pursuit of and commitment to everything that followed from the initial moment of divine disclosure that sets him apart and makes him an important model in this age in which pragmatism and practicality are so often praised.

When we think of Francis' relationship with nature, we inevitably think of him preaching to the birds. We should not forget that in the earliest account of that story (I Cel 58), some of the birds were scavengers. Francis loved creatures simply because they were God's handiwork rather than because they were beautiful to look at or useful to humanity. And for him, they were means for him to come to know and experience God. I think of the famous story of Father Flanigan encountering a boy carrying another child and exclaiming: "He ain't heavy, Father; he's my brother." Francis would say and mean that whether he were carrying a sibling or a stone or a sabre-toothed tiger. It is hard enough for most of us to shoulder the burden of trying to care for and defend our fellow humans who are in need. It seems an impossible burden to extend that same level of concern to include insects and swamps and shrubs. Yet, Francis shows us that we are called to carry that burden and that, as Christ promised, it is a light one (Mt 11:30).

An important part of Francis' genius was understanding the possibilities and limitations of academic study. Francis respected learning and theologians[6] and did not doubt their value to the cause of Christ. On the other hand, he knew that God's standard of judgment was not how much one knew about scripture but whether one lived according to its precepts. He feared that the subtlety of scholarly commentaries was often more to impress fellow scholars than to proclaim the truth. He knew that glosses provided excuses for people not to do what scripture called for. He hated hypocrisy more than anything, and scholars are particularly vulnerable to this sin because they often make a good case for a moral or theological position without being committed to living according to it. Furthermore, if only years of study can lead to the proper understanding of the gospel, then how can most of the human race live according to gospel precepts? Francis believed that all people could discover God and his will for humanity by experiencing creation and praying for forgiveness and grace. Francis calls all, and this is particularly relevant to scholars, to remember that God can be discovered in nature, in

[6]"And we should honor and respect all theologians," from Francis' "Testament" in *Francis and Clare: The Complete Works*, p. 154.

compassion, and in prayer at least as well as in books.

We live in an age of frenzied activity in which the contemplative life is often dismissed either as the vocation of a few monks and nuns or as an outdated elitist philosophy traceable to Plato and Aristotle. The world is so full of emergencies that demand immediate response from a Christian (starvation in Ethiopia, homelessness in American cities, natural disasters that kill people and destroy property) that many fall into the trap of following a Christian call to compassion that eventually fades because there is no time to re-examine the spiritual foundations of the original call. The magnitude of human needs combined with our inability to make much of an impact on their alleviation is an important cause of alienation and burnout; it is perhaps also a cause of what some perceive as the selfishness of today's youth. Some think that since they can do nothing to fight starvation and disease that has a measurable impact, they should at least try to provide for their own wellbeing. Francis' life offers alternatives. There is hope because we trust in God. If God has mercy on a sinner such as I, Francis suggests, then there is hope for all people. That is a fundamentally important Christian posture. Furthermore, Francis does not measure "success" statistically. There were probably as many miserable lepers and people without clothes and food at the time of his death as there were when he was alive. Francis was perceptive enough to realize that such a fact was not evidence that he had failed in his ministry to the wretched of the earth. The question for Francis was not whether he made an impact on the Umbrian poverty statistics but whether he had clothed those in need that he had come in contact with. It was *this* leper and *that* beggar that he served. Focusing on the details of ministry is difficult if not impossible without maintaining the perspective that it is God rather than one person who can renew the world.

The events that took place at Greccio and LaVerna are as extraordinary and important to us as they were to eyewitnesses. Some may have thought Francis mad for bringing animals and an empty crib near the altar at Greccio on that Christmas Eve of 1223. It was in one sense an audacious novelty. However, Francis was able to use those physical objects to make the incarnation "real" and immediate in the minds and hearts of many. Without experiencing the incarnation, it is impossible to experience Christ's death and thus his resurrection. Paul says in Romans 6 that we must die with Christ in order to have hope that we will rise with him; Francis knew that in order to die with Christ, one must experience fully his humanity. And as the paintings of the Christmas Crib at Greccio make clear, the Christ whom Francis mystically held in his arms that night is the same Christ visibly present to all in the mystery of the eucharist.[7]

That we must die with Christ is of course the meaning of LaVerna. No one may bypass the cross on the journey toward salvation. Only by embracing the cross and the suffering and sacrifice that it represents can one hope to share in the resurrection. Christians are often tempted to avoid the cross or at least to reduce the embrace to a symbolic gesture such as a few meatless days in Lent. The extraordinary event at LaVerna confirms a life that was a constant embrace of the cross. What did it mean for Francis to be constantly embracing the cross? It meant sacrificing his will to God. It included vulnerability to physical discomfort and sharing in the passion of Christ and of all those he came into contact with who were suffering. It included an intoxicating hope that more sober people would find ludicrous. Most important, embracing the cross is the great source of joy. Perhaps it is the joy of Francis that makes him so important because we see that a life of sacrifice, pain, and difficult ministry is a prerequisite for the greatest joy. No one ever died happier or more willingly than Francis of Assisi, and that is the most eloquent testimony of all to the quality of his life. If we cannot embrace Sister Death[8] as willingly as we embrace our other siblings, then we can never be truly joyful in the short time we inhabit the earth. Without hope and trust, death is to be feared and denied instead of being welcomed as a sister. There is no better way to summarize

[7]The early depictions of the Greccio story in Florence, Siena, and Assisi all emphasize the relationship of the crib to the altar, where the consecration took place shortly after Francis held the baby Jesus in his arms.

[8]The third part of Francis' "Canticle of the Creatures" includes praise of Sister Bodily Death; see *Francis and Clare: The Complete Works*, p. 39.

Francis' spiritual legacy than to end with a prayer which he did not write but which is often attributed to him; he is clearly its inspiration:

Lord, make me an instrument of your peace.
Where there is hatred, let me sow love,
Where there is injury, pardon,
Where there is doubt, faith,
Where there is despair, hope,
Where there is darkness, light,
Where there is sadness, joy.

O, Divine Master, grant that I may seek
not so much to be consoled as to console;
to be understood as to understand,
to be loved as to love,
for it is in giving that we receive,
it is in pardoning that we are pardoned,
and it is in dying that we are born to eternal life.
Amen

Bibliography

Obviously it is beyond the scope of this book to provide a comprehensive bibliography of works concerning St.Francis of Assisi, for they literally number in the thousands. What follows, therefore, is partial and slanted toward the particular issues concerning Francis that I have raised in this book. There are no citations to works not available in English.

A. BIBLIOGRAPHIES

In addition to bibliographies in many of the books cited below, the following one is of special value:

Brown, Raphael, compiler, "A Francis of Assisi Research Bibliography: Comprehensive for 1939-1969, Selective for Older Materials" in *St. Francis of Assisi: Omnibus of Sources* ed. Marion Habig. Chicago: Franciscan Herald Press, 1973, pp. 1667-1760. An earlier version of this bibliography, ending in the year 1963, appears in Omer Englebert, *Saint Francis of Assisi: A Biography* tr. Eva Marie Cooper. Chicago: Franciscan Herald Press, 2nd rev. English ed., 1965, pp. 493-607.

B. PRIMARY SOURCES FOR THE LIFE OF ST. FRANCIS

The *Omnibus* contains the best collection of primary materials in

English concerning the life of St. Francis. The volumes of the writings of Francis and Clare and of selected works by Bonaventure in the Paulist Press *The Classics of Western Spirituality* series are also of great value. Several early lives including the *Legenda Maior* have been translated in a volume in the Everyman's Library published in the United States by Dutton and in England by Dent. Complete citations to the volumes containing the sources for the life of St. Francis have already been given at the beginning of this book.

C. PRIMARY SOURCES RELEVANT TO THE LIFE OF ST. FRANCIS AND TO EARLY FRANCISCANISM

What follows here are sources from the thirteenth century written by Franciscans and about issues specifically related to Francis and his Order. Others are also cited at the beginning of this volume.

Apocalyptic Spirituality tr. and ed. Bernard McGinn. *The Classics of Western Spirituality*. Ramsey, NJ: Paulist Press, 1979.

Bonaventure. *The Disciple and the Master: St. Bonaventure's Sermons on St. Francis of Assisi* tr. Eric Doyle. Chicago: Franciscan Herald Press, 1983.

__________, *Rooted in Faith: Homilies to a Contemporary World* tr. Marigwen Schumacher. Chicago: Franciscan Herald Press, 1974.

__________, *Works* tr. Jose de Vinck, 5v. Paterson, NJ: St. Anthony Guild Press, 1960-1970

Jacopone da Todi. *The Lauds* tr. Serge and Elizabeth Hughes. *The Classics of Western Spirituality*. Ramsey, NJ: Paulist Press, 1982.

Meditations on the Life of Christ tr. Isa Ragusa and Rosalie Green. Princeton: Princeton University Press, 1961.

Salimbene de Adam. *The Chronicle* tr. Joseph Baird. *Medieval and Renaissance Texts and Studies*, #40. Binghamton, NY: Center for Medieval and Early Renaissance Studies, 1986.

D. STUDIES OF THE LIFE OF ST. FRANCIS

There are not only many biographies of St. Francis, but they are of many different types. The most comprehensive modern biography contains more than 2000 printed pages; on the other hand, many studies of the saint are primarily reflective and spiritual rather than historical. What follows must of necessity be only a sampling, and many good books are not cited here.

Armstrong, Edward. *Saint Francis: Nature Mystic.* Berkeley: University of California Press, 1973. This is an important study of Francis' nature mysticism by one who knows both the hagiographical tradition of Western Europe and a great deal of scientific information and lore about animals.

Bodo, Murray. *Francis: The Journey and the Dream.* Cincinnati: St.Anthony Messenger Press, 1972. A Franciscan writes in almost poetic rapture about Francis and his vision.

Boff, Leonardo. *Saint Francis: A Model for Human Liberation* tr. John Diercksmeier. New York: Crossroad, 1982. This biography is the work of one of South America's leading liberation theologians, and it approaches Francis' life from that perspective.

Chesterton, G.K. *St. Francis of Assisi.* Garden City, NY: Doubleday, 1924 (subsequent paperback editions in Doubleday's *Image Books* series). This is a classic look at Francis that has lost neither its charm nor its deep insights in the more than sixty years since its publication.

Cook, William. "Beatus Pacificus: Francis of Assisi as Peacemaker." *The Cord* 33 (1983): 130-136. Here is a brief essay about several stories concerning Francis bringing an end to violence and their meaning for our times.

Engelbert, Omer. *St. Francis of Assisi: A Biography* tr. Eva Marie Cooper. Chicago: Franciscan Herald Press, 1965 (subsequent paperback edition Ann Arbor: Servant Books, 1979). One of the great biographies of the saint in the twentieth century.

Fortini, Arnaldo. *Francis of Assisi* tr. Helen Moak. New York: Crossroad, 1981. This is an edited version of Fortini's massive biography of more than 2000 pages. Fortini was for many years mayor of Assisi and knew the city and the archives like no one before or since. The book has its quirks. Fortini in one passage will make a technical argument about property ownership derived from a close reading of surviving charters, and in the next passage "invent" or use his rather vivid imagination to recreate an event, going far beyond the sources. Nevertheless, this book is an indispensable starting point for studying Francis, and Helen Moak has done a great service in making it available to the English-speaking world.

Gasnick, Roy. *Francis, Brother of the Universe.* New York: Marvel Comics Group, 1980. This is probably the best selling version of Francis' life of all times—about half a million copies. It is well written (the author is a friar) and well drawn.

Ghilardi, Agostino. *The Life and Times of St. Francis* tr. Salvator Attanasio. New York: Paul Hamlyn, 1967. Although the text is not particularly insightful, this book contains many good photographs of places associated with Francis and of representations of Francis in paintings and manuscript illuminations.

Green, Julien. *God's Fool: The Life and Times of Francis of Assisi* tr. Peter Heinegg. London: Hodder and Stoughton, 1986. This is a highly acclaimed book that displays both passion and a lot of imagination in the recreation of Francis' life and thought.

Holl, Adolf. *The Last Christian: A Biography of Francis of Assisi* tr. Peter Heinegg. Garden City, NY: Doubleday, 1985. A somewhat eccentric but nevertheless insightful biography of the saint.

Jörgensen, Johannes. *St. Francis of Assisi* tr. T. O'Conor Sloane. Garden City, NY: Doubleday, 1955. This book was originally published in 1912 and has always been regarded as one of the finest studies of the saint, told with both good scholarship and great passion.

Moorman, John. *Saint Francis of Assisi.* London: SPCK, new ed. 1976. This is a brief but excellent account of the saint's life by a man who is both a great scholar of Franciscanism and also an Anglican bishop.

Nigg, Walter. *Francis of Assisi* tr. William Neil. Chicago: Franciscan Herald Press, 1975. This book contains a brief overview of Francis' life, but its main attraction is the wonderful photographs accompanied by selected texts from thirteenth-century sources.

Sabatier, Paul. *The Life of St. Francis of Assisi* tr. Louise Seymour Houghton. New York: Charles Scribner's Sons, 1894. This splendid piece of work is the starting point of modern scholarship on the life of St. Francis. Although many scholars today do not accept some of Sabatier's conclusions, this is a genuine classic that provides the reader great insight into the saint and also the best way into modern scholarship.

Smith, John Holland. *Francis of Assisi.* New York: Charles Scribner's Sons, 1972. Another fine biography, this one is especially valuable in examining Francis' life in the context of his times.

Sorrell, Roger. *St. Francis of Assisi and Nature.* New York: Oxford University Press, 1988. The subtitle, "Tradition and Innovation in Western Christian Attitudes Toward the Environment," is an excellent description of this significant book.

Zeffirelli, Franco. *Brother Sun, Sister Moon.* 1972. Released by Paramount Home Video, 1986. This attractive film takes a good deal of liberty with the early sources, and Francis at times appears to be a medieval hippie. Nevertheless, there is something appealing and enduring in this film.

E. STUDIES OF FRANCISCAN TEXTS AND THE FRANCISCAN ORDER IN THE THIRTEENTH CENTURY

Brooke, Rosalind. *The Coming of the Friars. Historical Problems: Studies and Documents*, #24. New York: Barnes and Noble, 1975. This book provides essential background and context and also a good description of the development of the Dominican Order. It also includes translations of documents not collected elsewhere.

__________, *Early Franciscan Government. Cambridge Studies in Medieval Life and Thought*, n.s. #7. Cambridge: Cambridge University Press, 1959. This is a fine scholarly study of the government of the Order before 1260 and is especially insightful concerning the generalate and personality of Brother Elias.

__________, "The Lives of St. Francis" in *Latin Biography* ed. T.A. Dorey. New York: Basic Books, 1967, p. 177-198. This article discusses several of the early biographies of Francis, and there is precious little material available in English about these lives. The author does not give due credit to the genius of the *Legenda Maior*.

Brown, Raphael. *The Roots of St. Francis*. Chicago: Franciscan Herald Press, 1981. This is a brief sketch of Umbria from earliest times with a focus on those elements of Umbrian history and geography that directly shaped Francis' life.

Cook, William. "Fraternal and Lay Images of St. Francis" in *Popes, Teachers, and Canon Law in the Middle Ages: Essays in Honor of Brian Tierney* ed. James Ross Sweeney and Stanley Chodorow. Ithaca: Cornell University Press, 1989. This essay shows that the written and visual accounts of Francis' life had different audiences and expressed different views of the saint and his Order.

__________, "Tradition and Perfection: Monastic Typology" in Bonaventure's *Life of St. Francis. The American Benedictine Review* 33 (1982): 1-20. This article examines how Bonaventure, in the *Legenda Maior*, used stories and even borrowed phrases from the lives of early monastic saints in order to place Francis in the tradition of monasticism.

————, and Ronald B. Herzman. *The Medieval World View: An Introduction.* New York: Oxford University Press, 1983. The book provides important background for the study of any medieval subject, and the last chapter is specifically concerned with Francis and the Order he founded.

Cousins, Ewert. *Bonaventure and the Coincidence of Opposites.* Chicago: Franciscan Herald Press, 1978. Cousins presents a masterful examination of the mystical theology of Bonaventure. He also suggests some implications of Bonaventure's thought for the twentieth century.

————, "Francis of Assisi: Christian Mysticism at the Crossroads" in *Mysticism and Religious Traditions* ed. Steven Katz. New York: Oxford University Press, 1983, pp. 163-190. This article is an important contribution to understanding Francis' mysticism and Bonaventure's attempt to demonstrate both its place in traditional Christian mystical thought and how it enlarges that tradition.

Daniel, Randolph. *The Franciscan Concept of Mission in the Middle Ages.* Lexington, KY: University of Kentucky Press, 1975. Daniel presents the reader with an understanding of Francis' own zeal to convert non-Christians and how this was interpreted by later Franciscan writers and missionaries.

Doyle, Eric. *St. Francis and the Song of Brotherhood.* New York: Seabury, 1981. Doyle reinterprets the "Canticle of the Creatures" in light of modern scientific thought, arguing that it provides much needed insight in the twentieth century. He even provides a modern version entitled "The Song of Sister Energy" in which God is praised through Brother DNA and Sister Nuclear Fusion.

Esser, Cajetan. *Origins of the Franciscan Order* tr. Aedan Daly and Irina Lynch. Chicago: Franciscan Herald Press, 1970. This is an important study of early Franciscanism by one of the greatest Franciscan scholars of the century.

Fleming, John. *An Introduction to the Franciscan Literature of the Middle Ages*. Chicago: Franciscan Herald Press, 1977. Fleming provides an intelligent and useful examination of the literature of the Franciscans from the early lives of the saint to vernacular literature that the movement inspired. As a great literary scholar, he provides an invaluable way of looking at a body of material all too rarely studied from a literary perspective. There is a fine chapter on "Bonaventure and the Themes of Franciscan Mysticism."

Hayes, Zachary. *The Hidden Center: Spirituality and Speculative Christology in St. Bonaventure*. Ramsey, NJ: Paulist Press, 1981. Although this book is in part technical, it is an important examination of the works of the greatest of all Franciscan writers.

Herzman, Ronald. "Dante and Francis." *Franciscan Studies* 42 (1982): 96-114. This essay is an important analysis of Dante's understanding of Francis, and especially Dante's version of Francis' life in *Paradiso* XI.

Kaftal, George. *St. Francis in Italian Painting*. London: George Allen and Unwin, 1950. This is a short, incomplete, and impressionistic treatment of the subject; but there is at present little else in English.

Lambert, Michael. *Franciscan Poverty*. London: SPCK, 1961. The meaning of Franciscan poverty became a central concern to the Order and the Church as a whole in the second half of the thirteenth century and the first half of the fourteenth. This book is the authoritative study of the issue.

Lapanski, Duane. *Evangelical Perfection: An Historical Examination of the Concept in the Early Franciscan Sources. Franciscan Institute Publications: Theology*

Series, #7. St. Bonaventure, NY: The Franciscan Institute, 1977. The author provides interesting background to the Franciscan idea of evangelical perfection as well as a study of the idea from pre-Bonaventuran sources.

Little, Lester. *Religious Poverty and the Profit Economy in Medieval Europe.* Ithaca: Cornell University Press, 1978. Little places Franciscan poverty in the context of the development of urban life and the evolution of a money economy. The author deals with how other religious orders attempted to deal with the new realities of urban life.

Moleta, Vincent. *From St. Francis to Giotto.* Chicago: Franciscan Herald Press, 1983. This is a useful examination of thirteenth-century Franciscanism, making use of paintings as well as written sources.

Moorman, John. *A History of the Franciscan Order from its Origins to the Year 1517.* Oxford: Clarendon Press,1968. Without a doubt, this is the most comprehensive and reliable account of the first three centuries of Franciscanism. Moorman's book is an important starting point for studying almost any topic relating to Francis and his Order.

Peters, Edward. "Restoring the Church and Restoring Churches: Event and Image in Franciscan Biography." *Franziskanische Studien* 68 (1986): 213-236. This article studies the story of Francis rebuilding San Damiano, San Pietro, and the Porziuncola in early written and visual texts.

Ratzinger, Joseph. *The Theology of History in St. Bonaventure* tr. Zachary Hayes. Chicago: Franciscan Herald Press, 1971.This is another seminal study of the writings of Bonaventure and thus important for the study of Franciscan thought in the thirteenth century.

Trexler, Richard. *Naked Before the Bishop: The Renunciation of Francis of Assisi in Literature and Art.* Forthcoming. In this soon-to-be-published monograph, a distinguished social historian examines the literary and visual representations of the story of Francis' renunciation and reexamines them in light of social and legal realities of the early thirteenth century.

F. PERIODICALS

There are numerous journals dedicated exclusively to Franciscan studies and literally thousands where one may find an occasional article concerning Francis or his Order. The Franciscan Institute at St. Bonaventure University in Olean, NY publishes two quite different journals. *Franciscan Studies* is a traditional academic journal. *The Cord* contains a great variety of material from scholarly studies to reflections and poems.

G. NOVELS

Eco, Umberto. *The Name of the Rose* tr. William Weaver. New York: Harcourt Brace Jovanovich, 1983. This recent bestseller set in the early fourteenth century weaves fiction with historical realities in a wonderful philosophical murder mystery. The question of the meaning of apostolic poverty that pitted the friars against Pope John XXII in the 1320s is a central issue in Eco's novel. Most of that Franciscan context is lost in the film version.

Kazantzakis, Nikos. *Saint Francis* tr. P.A. Bien. New York: Simon and Schuster, 1962. This novel is a moving account of the saint's life. Written as a first person narrative of Brother Leo, it describes with great intensity the struggle of Francis to be like Christ and of Leo to be like Francis. This translation was republished in England by Bruno Cassirer under the title *God's Pauper: St. Francis of Assisi.*